DEDICATION

This book is dedicated to the Hawaiian people and to the aloha spirit. May they both endure.

HIKING OAHU

The Capital Isle

Robert Smith

Wilderness Press
BERKELEY

First edition September 1978
Second edition September 1980
Third edition July 1983
Revised second printing July 1987

Maps by Kevin G. Chard
Cover photo by the author
Design by Thomas Winnett

Library of Congress Card Catalog Number 83-50380
International Standard Book Number 0-89997-033-8

Manufactured in the United States

Published by Wilderness Press
2440 Bancroft Way
Berkeley, California 94704
(415) 843-8080

Write for free catalog

ACKNOWLEDGEMENTS

Many people made significant contributions to this book. Thanks to Bill Crane for his companionship on many of the hikes and for his knowledge and helpful suggestions. Thanks also to Fred Samia, who assisted by reading the manuscript. I am indebted to Louis Mellencamp, who contributed professional advice and assistance on the photos included in this volume. A special mahalo to Nancy, my wife, for typing the manuscript.

Photo credits

Robert Smith: pages 19, 27, 31, 41, 50, 55, 57, 61, 69, 89, 91, 95, 98, 102, 106
Thomas Winnett: pages ii, 7, 25, 35, 37, 74
Bob Immler: page viii

Other books by Robert Smith
from Wilderness Press

Hiking Kauai: the Garden Isle
Hiking Maui: the Valley Isle
Hiking Hawaii: the Big Island
Hawaii's Best Hiking Trails

Contents

Northern Oahu shore

Part I: Introduction

Oahu

Hiking Areas ⬜

The Island

Take a walk along Waikiki Beach any time of the day, any time of the year, and you will understand why this, the third largest of the Hawaiian Islands, is called Oahu, "the gathering place": Everyone is here— Japanese, Chinese, Filipinos, Blacks, Samoans, Germans, Canadians, Australians and others.

What is it that brings people here from all over the world? Can it be the air temperature, which seldom varies by more than 10 degrees, with a year-round average of 75°F? Can it be the 80° water temperature at Waikiki Beach? Can it be the enchantment of precipitous cliffs and heavily overgrown valleys existing as backdrops to a city covered with asphalt and high-rise buildings? Can it be the fascinating blend of the multi-ethnic population? Can it be the life style in which individuality reigns supreme, and muumuus and cutoffs, oxfords and bare feet, tuxedoes and swimsuits intermingle in the restaurants and discotheques? Can it be the surf, the music, the suntanned bodies, the aloha spirit, the wild fruits, the hiking, the camping, the slow pace of life, the . . . . ?

The truth is that Waikiki, and Honolulu, are all of these things. The truth is that long before the first-time visitor arrives, Hawaii has transmitted its message via the plaudits of happy visitors, the media, and the Hawaii Visitors Bureau. The truth is that the first-time visitor has been primed for pleasure long before his jumbo 747 flies over Diamond Head and lands in Honolulu. For most people, there are no disappointments, and they return again and again.

Indeed, the crowds are sometimes so great that people spill off the sidewalk onto Kalakaua Avenue in order to get by casual strollers. Combine the 3-million-plus tourists who visit Oahu annually with the 805,000 permanent residents (over 80% of the state's population) and you have a lot of people on a rather small island.

Honolulu was not an original Hawaiian city. It was established by the followers of Captain Cook who, in search of anchorage, discovered this protected deep-water bay. Honolulu (lit., "protected bay") grew rapidly and was soon recognized as the trading and business center of the islands by King Kamehameha III. The official capital of the Kingdom of Hawaii was moved from Lahaina, Maui, to Honolulu in 1850. For the next 85 years, the southeast end of the city remained a swamp where taro was cultivated and ducks and other marsh birds roamed freely. However, in the past 40 years Waikiki has been dramatically altered from its humble beginnings to become one of the most recognized beaches in the world.

But there is more to Oahu than world-famous Waikiki, Diamond Head and Pearl Harbor. On the windward (east) side of the island are the Hawaiian communities of Hauula and Laie, where numerous valley hikes and beach camping, away from the crowds, awaits the outdoors person. The north shore of Oahu may well be the surfing capital of the world, with the Banzai Pipeline, Sunset Beach and Waimea Bay, but it is also the departure point for hikes to a number of peaks along the Waianae mountain range. And lastly, there are the central plains, where most of the island's pineapple and sugar cane are grown, and where the trailheads are located for hikes up to the Koolau mountain range for striking panoramas of the island.

The two mountain ranges and the island of Oahu were created by volcanic eruptions. Oahu took shape as subsequent lava flows filled the area between the ranges until the present 607 square miles remained. In time, the Koolau mountain range on the east side and the Waianae mountain range on the west side were further sculpted by natural forces, so that both have gently sloping parts and steep precipitous areas.

Although there are no hikes on Oahu to compare to the Kalalau Trail on Kauai, the trails in Haleakala Crater on Maui or the Mauna Loa Trail to the 13,680-foot summit on Hawaii, there are trails to excite and to challenge the hiker. The Dupont Trail to Mt. Kaala, the highest point (4025 feet) on Oahu, is an outstanding hike, and the hikes to Sacred Falls and into Poamoho Valley are equal to any of the valley hikes on the other islands.

Using This Book

While most of the hikes on Oahu are short-distance, part-day hikes, I have included a wide selection of trips from short, easy family walks to long, difficult hikes. Many of the hikes are on public lands where well-maintained trails direct the hiker. Other hikes are on private land—pineapple and sugar-cane holdings—and some are on military reservations. In spite of the time and effort required to secure permission from property owners, I have included these worthy hikes. For example, the Poamoho Ridge Trail (Hiking Area No. 21) is a noble hike, but it requires permission from the State Division of Forestry, the US Army, the Dole Pineapple Co. and the Wailua Sugar Company! I have not included areas from which hikers are forbidden by law (protected watershed) or where the terrain is dangerous and unsafe even though local people may boast of their adventures into these places. Each year numerous injuries and some fatalities occur where people have hiked in spite of the prohibition. For example, a prominent sign at the end of the Manoa Falls Trail (Hiking Area No. 6) warn hikers not to climb above the falls, where the terrain is brittle and treacherous. Nevertheless, numerous injuries, rescues, and even deaths have been recorded there in recent years. In the first nine months of 1977, four hikers died on Oahu! However, good judgment and a regard for the time-tested rules of hiking are good protection.

In order to ensure a safe and enjoyable experience and to protect the environment, remember:

1. Do not hike alone.
2. Many Hawaiian trails are wet and slippery, and the terrain is loose and brittle.
3. Contrary to popular belief, it is not possible to live off the land. Carry your own food.
4. Although some fruits are available, never eat or taste unknown fruits or plants.
5. Carry your own water or purify water from streams.
6. A tent with a rain fly ensures comfortable and dry nights.
7. Carry your trash out.
8. Bury personal waste away from streams.
9. Firewood in most places is not available or is too wet for use. Carry a stove for cooking.
10. Darkness begins right after sunset.

In planning a hike, the reader is advised to consult the Hiking Chart below in order to give due consideration to driving time, hiking time, and the clothing and supplies necessary. I have rated all the hikes and placed them in one of four categories. A "family" rated hike is for those who are looking for short, easy hikes. The "hardy family" classification requires a degree of effort and sound physical condition. Both the strenuous and the difficult hikes require a measure of endurance, since they are longer hikes and most of them involve a considerable gain in altitude. They also require good footwear and more equipment.

Obviously, hiking time varies from person to person, depending on such factors as pace and the extent to which one chooses to linger for lunch and to swim where pools exist. The time noted in the Hiking Chart is based on a leisurely pace. Trail distance is based either on an exact measurement or on an approximation with the aid of a topographic map.

Driving time and mileage cited are based on the posted speed limit and are measured from Waikiki.

Specific driving instructions precede each hike description.

The equipment noted on the Hiking Chart is minimal for hiking enjoyment. As a rule, however, I always carry water, food and a first-aid kit. Although the choice between tennis shoes and hiking boots is listed in some cases as optional, I prefer hiking boots in most cases. Obviously, your feet are an important consideration in hiking since it is common, on an island that has experienced extensive volcanic activity, to have volcanic ash or rock underfoot. Usually, shorts or long pants are optional, except where the brush is thick or when the weather requires warmer clothing.

Drinking water is available from streams in many areas, but it should be boiled or treated, since cattle, pigs and goats may share the water supply. To avoid the chance of illness, carry one quart of water per person. In many areas, firewood is at a premium. A small, light, reliable backpacking stove is a convenience and a comfort if you plan to cook out.

Before each hike description you will find the hike rating, trail features, hiking distance and time, specific driving instructions, instructions for getting there by bus and introductory notes. On some hikes it is necessary to walk on private property. Information and addresses are provided so that you can secure permission in advance. Permission is usually readily granted either over the telephone or in person when you sign a liability waiver.

In the trail narrative I usually mention the flora and fauna to be seen along the way, especially the unusual and the unique, in an effort to add to your hiking enjoyment. But I don't mention everything, and you may wish to buy one of several guides to plants and animals of the islands, available at many stores. I recommend *Tropical Trees of Hawaii* and

Hawaii Blossoms both by Dorothy and Bob Hargreaves and *Hawaii's Birds* by the Hawaii Audubon Society.

Preceding each trail narrative is a map that will help you find the trailhead and to locate trail highlights. The maps show many features of the hikes as well as campsites.

The fine public transportation system on Oahu deserves a special note. Many visitors make the mistake of renting a car when "The Bus"—yes that's what it's called—is convenient, reliable, comfortable and inexpensive. The Bus makes regular stops at most places of interest on the island. Unquestionably, The bus is the best bargain on Oahu. For 60¢ you can ride nearly 100 miles around the island: From Honolulu, The Bus travels along the east coast, passes across the north shore and returns through the central portion of Oahu to Honolulu. The system is so reliable that I have included instructions for taking The Bus to the trailheads.

The one shortcoming of the system is that backpacks are not allowed unless they can be carried on the lap or stored under the seat. Call 531-1611 from 5:30 a.m. to 10 p.m. daily for information and schedules.

An unusual condition exists throughout Hawaii regarding highway numbers. Pick up five highway maps of the Islands and the chances are good that they will not show the same highway numbers. In this book, on the maps and in the driving instructions for each hike, I have used the route number posted on the highway. In some instances, I have made note of this problem in the driving instructions.

Hiking Area Number	Hiking Chart	Hike Rating				Trail Time			From Waikiki		Equipment					Features				
		Family	Hardy Family	Strenuous	Difficult	Distance (miles) (L indicates loop)	Time (hours)	Gain in feet	Miles	Time (hours)	Raingear	Boots	Tennis Shoes	Carry Water	Take Food	Swimming	Waterfalls	Views	Historical Sites	Fruits
1	Diamond Head	X				.7	1	550	4	¼			X	X	X			X	X	
2	Black Point	X				1	½		3	¼						X				
3	Old Pali Highway	X				.3	¼		7	¼			X					X	X	X
4	Judd Memorial	X				1.3L	1		6	¼			X	X		X		X		
5	Makiki/Tantalus								3	¼										
	Kanealole	X				.7	½	500				X		X	X			X		X
	Nahuina		X			.6	½	600				X		X	X			X		
	Makiki Valley	X				1.1	1					X		X	X			X		X
	Makiki Branch A	X				.7	½	500				X		X	X					
	Moleka		X			.5	½	460				X		X	X			X		X
	Ualakaa	X				.6	½					X		X	X			X		
6	Manoa Falls	X				.8	1	800	3	¼		X		X		X	X			X
	Aihualama		X			1.4	1½	400				X		X				X		
7	Waahila Ridge		X			2	2	700	4	¼		X		X	X			X	X	
8	Lanipo			X		3	3	1600	6	½	X			X	X			X		
9	Wiliwilinui			X		3	3	2000	10	½	X			X	X			X		
10	Hanauma Bay								12	½										
11	Kahana Valley	X				4.5	2½		26	1	X	X	X	X	X	X		X		X
	Koko Head	X				1	½	450				X		X	X			X		
	Koko Crater			X		1	1	1000				X		X	X			X	X	
	Blowhole	X				2	1½					X		X	X	X		X		
12	Puu Piei			X		.8	1	1700	26	1	X			X				X		
13	Sacred Falls	X				2.2	1¼		28	1¼		X		X	X	X	X			X
14	Hauula								30	1¼										
	Hauula	X				2.5L	1¼	600				X		X	X			X		
	Maakua Gulch			X		3	3	1100			X	X		X	X	X	X			
	Papali	X				2.5L	2	800				X		X	X			X		
15	Laie			X		3	3	1400	36	1½	X			X	X	X	X	X		X
16	Aiea Loop	X				4.8L	3		12	½	X	X	X	X	X			X		X
17	Waimano				X	7.1	4	1600	14	½	X	X		X	X	X		X		
18	Manana				X	6	4	1700	15	½	X	X		X	X	X		X		
19	Wahiawa			X		4	3	650	22	1	X	X	X	X	X	X		X		
20	Poamoho Valley	X				3	2	1000	22	1	X	X	X	X	X	X	X			
21	Poamoho Ridge			X		3.4	3	800	28	1½	X	X		X	X			X		
22	Dupont				X	4	5	3800	30	1½	X	X		X	X			X		
23	Kaneaki Heiau			X		.5	½	1900	36	1½	X								X	X
24	Kuakalo			X		4.5L	3	500	41	2	X			X	X	X	X			X
25	Kaena Point	X				2	1½		42	2			X	X	X	X				

9

Camping

Hiking can be an exciting way to see Oahu, and camping can make your visit an inexpensive one. Since camping is a popular activity with local people, make your plans in advance and obtain permits as soon as you arrive on the island. There are three state and two private campgrounds on the island and numerous county beach parks where camping is permitted. Camping is free at the state and county parks. At one (Kakela) of the private campgrounds the fee (1986) is $5.00 per person over 12 years old while the second (Hukilau) is free.

Camping is permitted at three campgrounds in the state park system on Oahu. The campground at Keaiwa Heiau State Park is in a shaded, wooded area near the trailhead of the Aiea Loop Trail (Hiking Area No. 16). Malaekahana State Park is just north of Laie on the east coast of Oahu. The campground is located on a beautiful white, sandy beach. It is a new park and campground with new facilities. Sand Island State Park campground is located on an island in Honolulu Bay. It is a popular and hence crowded recreational area. Reservations are required, and camping permits are limited from Fridays through Tuesdays only. Reservations may be made by mail, but the applications must be received by the Department of State Parks at least seven calendar days in advance of the date the permit is to be in effect. (All addresses are in the appendix.)

The City of Honolulu operates 63 recreational areas located on all parts of the island. Camping is permitted at 15 places, all of which are beach parks.

Permits are not issued earlier than two weeks before
the day of occupancy. Camping is allowed from Fridays
through Tuesdays only. Permits can be obtained from the
Department of Parks and Recreation in Honolulu or at
any of 10 satellite city halls located around the island. (All
addresses are in the appendix.) All the campgrounds have
cold-water showers, drinking water and restrooms. Most
of the beach parks receive heavy use, so they are not
always clean and the facilities are not always all in good
operating order. The campgrounds at Waimanalo, Swanzy,
Kahana Bay, Punaluu, Mokuleia, Keaau, Lualualei, Nana-
kuli and Kahe are recommended, since they are usually
clean and they have ample space for camping. Trailer
camping is permitted at all of the parks where tents are
allowed except Lualualei Beach Park and at Kaaawa
Beach Park. Trailers must be self-contained, since there
are no electrical or sewer connections.

Zions Securities (address in Appendix) in Laie operates two private beach campgrounds—Kakela and Hukilau. Both are satisfactory if the state and county parks are
not available. Permits can be obtained at their office in
Laie. A fee of $5.00 (1986) per person over 12 years old is
charged at Kakela. There is no fee to use Hukilau since it
does not have any facilities.

The camper should keep in mind that most of the
campsites on Oahu are in heavily populated areas or
in areas accessible to population centers. Consequently, all of the ills—thievery, damage to equipment,
drunkenness—of urban living are present. Campers
should not leave valuables and equipment unattended
or unprotected.

Food and Equipment

The following equipment is recommended for day hikes.

Knapsack
Hiking boots, strong shoes, or tennis shoes
Canteen, quart size (one per person)
Scout or Swiss Army knife
Insect repellent
Shorts
Bathing suit
Sunburn lotion and/or preventive
Sun glasses
Whistle for each child
Camera and film
Hiking Oahu—The Capital Isle
Hat
Optional:
    Poncho or raingear
    Towel
    Waterproof matches
    Flashlight

Planning and preparation are particularly important for the backpacker. The following equipment is recommended for overnight hikes and for campers.

BACKPACK CHECKLIST
General Equipment:
    Frame and pack
    Lightweight sleeping bag or blanket
    Tube tent or nylon tent with rain fly—rain is common in most areas
    Plastic ground cover—the ground is damp in most areas
    Sleep pad
    Canteen, quart size
    Scout or Swiss Army knife
    Flashlight
    40 feet of nylon cord
    First-aid kit

Cooking Gear
  Backpack stove
  Fuel
  Cooking pots
  Sierra cup
  Waterproof matches

Clothing
  Poncho or raingear—A MUST
  Pants
  Shorts and/or bathing suit
  Hat or bandana
  Undershorts
  T-shirts
  Socks
  Hiking boots

Toilet Articles
  Soap (biodegradable)
  Toothbrush/powder-paste
  Part-roll toilet paper
  Chapstick
  Comb
  Washcloth and towel
  Insect repellent
  Sunburn lotion or preventive

Miscellaneous
  Sun glasses
  Camera and film
  Plastic bags
  Fishing gear

Hawaiian Made Easy

For your interest, throughout the text wherever a Hawaiian place name is used, I have provided a literal translation if possible. In many instances, Hawaiian names have multiple meanings and even the experts sometimes disagree over the literal meaning. The meanings given here are based on the best information available and on the context in which the name is used. As students of the environment, the Hawaiians had a flair for finding the most expressive words to describe their physical surroundings.

Most visitors are reluctant to try to pronounce Hawaiian words. But with a little practice and a knowledge of some simple rules, you can develop some language skill and add to your Hawaiian experience. Linguists regard Hawaiian as one of the most fluid and melodious languages of the world. There are only 12 letters in the Hawaiian alphabet: five vowels, a,e,i,o,u, and seven consonants, h,k,l,m,n,p,w. Hawaiian is spelled phonetically. Correct pronunciation is easy if you do not try to force English pronunciation onto the Hawaiian language. Vowel sounds are simple: a=ah; e=eh; i=ee; o=oh; and u=oo. Consonant sounds are the same as in English with the exception of w. Rules for w are not adhered to with any consistency by local people. Generally, w is pronounced "w" at the beginning of a word and after a. For example, Waimea is pronounced "Wai-may-ah" and wala-wala is "Wah-lah-wah-lah." Hawaiians also usually pronounce w as "w" when it follows o or u: auwaha is "ah-oo-wah-hah," and hoowali is "hoh-oh-wah-lee." When w is next to the final letter of a word, it is variably pronounced "w" and "v"; Wahiawa is "wah-he-ah-wa," but Hawi is "ha-vee." Listen to the locals for their treatment of this sound. Since the Hawaiian language is not strongly accented, the visitor will probably be understood without employing any accent.

Part II:
Hiking Trails on Oahu

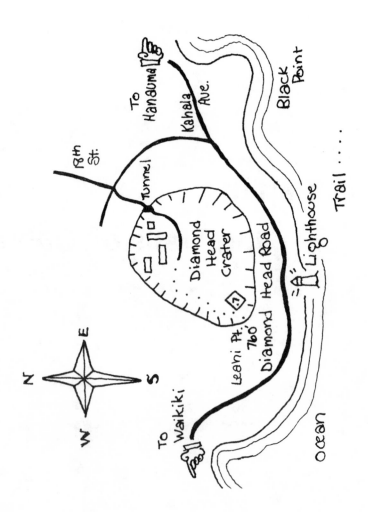

DIAMOND HEAD

(Hiking Area No. 1)

Rating: Family.

Features: Panorama of greater Honolulu area, historical site, extinct volcanic crater.

Permission: None.

Hiking Distance & Time: .7 miles, 1 hour, 550-foot gain.

Driving Instructions: From Honolulu (4 miles, ¼ hour) drive south on Kalakaua Ave., right on Diamond Head Road and around to east side of crater, left at sign marked "Diamond Head Crater" opposite 18th St. Follow road through tunnel into crater to parking area on left.

Bus Instructions: From Waikiki on Kalakaua Ave. take bus #58 (Sea Life Park) to 18th St. and Diamond Head road at a sign marked "Diamond Head Crater." Follow the road into the crater.

Introductory Notes: Although the hike to the summit of Diamond Head is hot and dry, the panorama offered from the top and along the rim trail is striking. This is a "must" hike for the whole family. Although a large portion of the crater and the surrounding area are on a military reservation, the hiking trail is under the jurisdiction of the Division of State Parks.

Without question, Diamond Head is the most photographed and the most readily identifiable place in Hawaii. Before the arrival of Western man, the area was known as Leahi (lit., "casting point"). In the early 1800's British sailors found calcite crystals in the rocks on the slopes of the crater and thought they were diamonds. Following the discovery, the tuff crater was called Kaimana-Hila (lit., "Diamond Hill"), and today the world-famous place is known as Diamond Head. Geologists estimate that the crater was formed some 100,000 years ago by violent steam explosions. During World War II Diamond Head was an important bastion for the protection of the island. Gun emplacements, lookout towers, and tunnels were concealed in and on the walls of the crater. Although abandoned in recent years, these places are interesting to investigate, particularly for children. It is helpful to carry a flashlight, since the trail passes through two short tunnels and up a spiral stairway.

On the Trail: The trailhead on the northwest side of the parking area is marked, and the trail is easy to follow to the summit. Kiawe (*Prosopis pallida*) trees abound on the floor of the crater. These valuable trees with fernlike leaves and thorny branches are the descendants of a single seed planted by Father Bachelot, a priest, in 1828 in his churchyard in Honolulu. The tree is a source not only of fuel and lumber but also of honey (produced from the flower), medicine, tannin and fodder, which is produced from its beanlike yellow pods containing 25% grape sugar.

As you continue along the gently rising trail to the first concrete landing and lookout, you should be able to identify a number of birds. Two species of doves, the barred dove (*Geopelia striata*) and the spotted dove (*Streptopelia chinensis*), are common and abundant on Oahu. The spotted dove, the larger of the two, has a band of black around the sides and back of the neck which is spotted with white. The barred dove is pale brown above, gray below, and barred with black. You should also see the beautiful, bright red, male cardinal (*Richmondena cardinalis*) with its orange beak and black face.

The concrete landing is the first of many lookout points along the trail. You have a good view of the crater and are able to distinguish some of the bunkers and gun emplacements on the slopes and on the crest of the crater. Follow the steps and the pipe railing to the first tunnel. You cannot see daylight at the end of the tunnel, because it turns to the left at midpoint. A flashlight is not necessary to pass through the tunnel safely, but it is a comfort to small children since it *is* dark. As you leave the tunnel, investigate the rooms in the concrete building opposite the exit, which were used for supplies and contained a power unit. Look for the bunker behind the building and hike to the left to a viewpoint overlooking the crater. A steep staircase—99 steps—leads the hiker into a short tunnel at the end of which is an observation room and the first view of Waikiki and the greater Honolulu area. Look for the room containing a spiral stairway. Climb

Waikiki from inside bunker atop Leahi Point

the stairway and then the ladder which takes you to the top and to the summit of Diamond Head. The concrete building at the summit is situated on top of Leahi Point at an elevation of 760 feet. Keep a watchful eye on children, for the summit's flanks are precipitous. The observation point at the summit provides a shady and comfortable picnic spot as well as a panoramic view.

It is possible to hike completely around the rim of the crater and to return to the parking lot by cutting through the brush, but the trail is steep and dangerous due to loose volcanic rock and ash. Only confident hikers should attempt this alternative route to the parking area. You will find numerous observation points and gun emplacements around the rim similar to those at the summit.

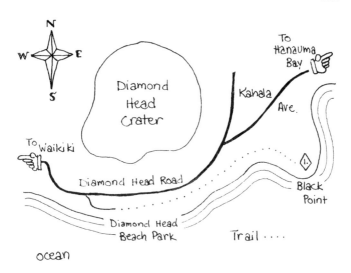

BLACK POINT

(Hiking Area No. 2)

Rating: Family.

Features: Beach hike, tidepools, swimming, good surfing for beginners (2-5 feet).

Permission: None.

Hiking Distance & Time: 1 mile, ½ hour.

Driving Instructions: From Honolulu (3 miles, ¼ hour) drive south on Kalakaua Ave., then right on Diamond Head Road to Diamond Head Beach Park or to a parking turnout off the road overlooking the beach.

Bus Instructions: From Waikiki take bus #14 (Maunalani Heights) to Diamond Head Beach Park. Walk to the beach and trailhead.

Introductory Notes: Hiking the shoreline anywhere in Hawaii is a delight for the whole family. Swimming and surfing are good at Diamond Head Beach, so there are a lot of wahines ("girls") and kanes ("boys") on the beach. There are also other interesting beach sights, such as tidepools.

On the Trail: Begin the hike anywhere along Diamond Head Beach Park and walk east. The Diamond Head Lighthouse to the west marks the finish line for the annual Trans-Pac Yacht Race. The surf is rated good by locals, and the beach is less crowded than Waikiki. The cliffs bordering the beach provide a barrier from the noise and the crowds of Honolulu. Haalawai (lit., "the water basalt") Beach at the midpoint of the hike is rated as a safe swimming beach. It is a good place to relax, to picnic, and to watch the surfers and other beach sights. Hike out to Kupikipikio (lit., "rough") Point, or Black Point, as it is more commonly called, for tidepools and for some interesting lava formations shaped by the crashing sea. Black Point is a place where you can spend a few relaxing hours or a full day only a short distance from one of the most crowded beaches in the world.

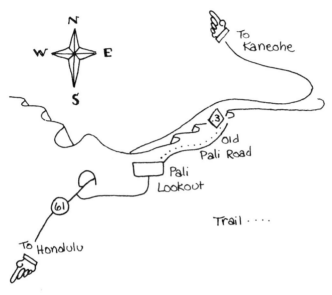

OLD PALI HIGHWAY

(Hiking Area No. 3)

Rating: Family.

Features: Superb views of east side, historical site.

Permission: None.

Hiking Distance & Time: .3 miles, ¼ hour.

Driving Instructions: From Honolulu (7 miles, ¼ hour) drive northwest on H-1, then right on Route 61 (Pali Highway) and follow signs to Pali Lookout.

Bus Instructions: No bus service to Nuuanu Pali Lookout.

Introductory Notes: While Diamond Head is probably the most photographed place on Oahu, the Nuuanu Pali (lit., "cool height cliff") is probably the most visited. The Nuuanu Pali offers a stunning view of the east side; it is a place of historical importance, and it is a spot where very strong winds return objects thrown by visitors. From the lookout and along the short trail, the broad panorama of the east side spans from Lanikai in the southeast to Kailua and Kaneohe below the Pali to Kahaluu in the north. The distinctive Mokapu (lit., "taboo district") Peninsula to the northeast is the place, according to Hawaiian legend, where man was created. Some believe that the four great gods, Kane, Kanaloa, Ku and Lono, met here. Kane and Kanaloa made images of themselves in the dirt and then argued over which one had the power to create man. While Kanaloa's image turned to stone, Kane's image came to life and became a man after Kane said "Come alive," and Ku and Lono responded, "Live." Kane's man was named Wakea, and some believe he was the ancestor of all Hawaiians. As Wakea walked, he noticed that his shadow always followed him. When he awoke the next morning, he found a beautiful woman lying by his side. He thought that the gods had changed his shadow into a woman, so he called her Keakuahulilani, "the shadow made of heaven."

Nuuanu Pali is the site of a significant and tragic battle that took place in 1795, the year in which Kamehameha the Great added Oahu to his kingdom. His forces drove the Oahu warriors up to the Pali and overwhelmed them. One account records that 300 warriors were driven over the cliff by Kamehameha's forces. Another story says that the defeated army jumped to its death rather than surrender.

On the Trail: This short trail begins on an 1,186-foot-high perch in the Kaneohe Forest Reserve known as the Nuuanu Pali Lookout. At the Pali, there is a break in the Koolau (lit., "windward") Mountain Range that has given Honolulu travelers a route to the east side for hundreds of years. Originally a footpath, it was made a horse trail in 1845 and later widened to accommodate carriages. Today a modern highway and a tunnel through the mountain speed travelers over the pali. A ramp to the right of the lookout leads to the old Pali Road. Gale-force winds prevent easy passage to the road, so hold on to all that you value! There is no wind on the old road, so pause frequently to enjoy and to photograph the fluted palisades and the richly foliated 3000-foot peaks of the Koolau Range. It is a breath-taking sight, for the mountains drop abruptly to the valley, and the pasture land below stretches to the sea.

Proceed down the road with some caution, since the road is wet and slippery in places, and falling rocks and boulders present a hazard. Look for a small stream on the right a few hundred yards from the lookout. Walk up the stream a short distance to a small waterfall and a delightful place to picnic.

JUDD MEMORIAL

(Hiking Area No. 4)

Rating: Family.

Features: Swimming, mud-sliding, introduced flora.

Permission: None.

Hiking Distance & Time: 1.3 mile loop, 1 hour.

Driving Instructions: From Honolulu (6 miles, ¼ hour, drive northwest on H-1, right on Route 61 (Pali Highway), right on Old Pali Highway, right on Nuuanu Pali Drive for .7 mile to Reservoir No. 2 spillway just before bridge marked "1931".

Bus Instructions: From Waikiki take bus #4 (Nuuanu-Dowsett) to Nuuanu Pali Drive/Kimo Drive. Walk up Nuuanu Pali Drive to the trailhead.

Introductory Notes: The hike to the Jackass-ginger pool in Nuuanu Stream is an easy and delightful outing for the family—even though mosquitoes are plentiful. Be certain to take old clothes, lunch, insect repellent, and a piece of plastic for mud-sliding.

On the Trail: The trail begins east of the spillway and downhill from the road and reaches Nuuanu (lit., "cool height") Stream after a few hundred feet. Large stream rocks make a convenient bridge to cross the stream, but do so with caution. Across the stream the trail enters a bamboo thicket, climbs into a eucalyptus grove, and continues into a stand of Norfolk Island pines (*Araucaria excelsa*). Native to Norfolk Island near Australia, these perfectly symmetrical evergreens were introduced to the Islands to be used as windbreaks and for timber. The smaller trees are used locally as Christmas trees. Designated as

Jackass ginger pool

the Charles S. Judd Memorial Grove in 1953, this forest of planted trees was so named in honor of the first "local boy" Territorial Forester. There are numerous mudsliding chutes in the area where it is possible, when they are wet, to toboggan down the hill on a plastic sheet, on pili grass or on ti leaves. The latter was the traditional Hawaiian conveyance. Mud-sliding is an ancient Hawaiian sport particularly popu-lar with Hawaiian royalty. Look for a wet place and give it a try. The nearby stream is a convenient place to wash off the mud.

The trail follows the forest-reserve boundary near a residential area and then turns downhill toward Nuuanu Stream through a maze of guava and hau brush. A short distance from this dense thicket, the trail passes above the Jackass-ginger pool. From here, a number of spur trails and mud-sliding chutes lead to the pool below. Don't miss the pool and a chance to swim and picnic.

To return to the trailhead, retrace your steps up the hillside to the point from which you descended and continue southeast and then north (left) along the initial portion of the trail which will return you to the road. A shorter route to the trailhead goes north from the pool through the bushes a short dis-tance to the Nuuanu Pali Drive. Once on the road, walk east (right) to the trailhead.

MAKIKI/TANTALUS

(Hiking Area No. 5)

Rating: See individual hikes.

Features: Mountain apples, Job's tears, native and introduced flora, valley views.

Permission: None

Hiking Distance & Time: See individual hikes.

Driving Instructions:

> *To Makiki Valley* From Honolulu (3 miles, ¼ hour) drive up Makiki St., turn left on Makiki Heights Dr. and continue straight on paved drive in Forestry "baseyard" (2135 Makiki Heights Dr.). Drive past a sign "Makiki Forest Recreation Area" to a parking area on the right just before a chain gate.

> *To Tantalus* From Honolulu (6 miles, ¼ hour) drive up Makiki Street, turn left on Makiki Heights Dr., then go right on Tantalus. Drive three miles to the top, where there are a telephone-service road on the left and a trailhead marker.

Bus Instructions:

> *To Makiki Valley* From Waikiki on Kuhio Ave. take bus #2 ("Liliha-Puunui" or "School-Middle St.") to Beretania/Alapai St. Secure a transfer and walk toward the ocean to Hotel St. Take bus #15 (Pacific Heights) to Mott-Smith Dr. and walk toward the mountains to Makiki Heights Dr. and to the trailhead.

> *To Tantalus* No bus service on Tantalus Drive or Round Top Drive.

Introductory Notes: There are three trails in Makiki Valley, two trails in the Tantalus area, two trails that connect the Tantalus area with Makiki Valley, one trail that joins Makiki Valley with Puu Ualakaa State Park, and one trail that connects Tantalus with Manoa Valley (see map). Consequently, there are trails to suit most hikers' interests and abilities. Your choices should be easy after consulting the maps and the trail narratives.

Tantalus and Round Top drives combine to make a popular auto tour above Honolulu. The many turnouts, which provide panoramas of Honolulu, are favorites of visitors and locals in the daytime and lovers in the evening. The two hikes that lead into the mountains from the top of the road are a delight for

the whole family. Local students named this area
"Tantalus" after the mythical Greek king. Tantalus
Mountain (2013 feet) was so named, it is suggested,
because as the students hiked, the peak seemed to
recede. (You may recall that Tantalus was punished
by being made to stand in a pool of water that re-
ceded each time he tried to drink.)

You have a choice of numerous trailheads for the
hikes included in this area. I suggest that you begin
your hiking either at the Manoa Cliffs trailhead on
Tantalus Drive or at the Puu Ohia trailhead, where
Tantalus Drive becomes Round Top Drive (0.5 mile
from the Manoa Cliffs trailhead on Tantalus Drive).
The Manoa Cliffs trailhead on Round Top Drive is on
the mountain side of the road at telephone pole #55
opposite a turnout and parking area. Two other good
choices of trailheads are the Aihualama trailhead near
the base of Manoa Falls in Manoa Valley and the
Makiki Valley trailhead.

**Kanealole Trail, 0.7 mile one-way, ½ hour (trail rat-
ing: family). Elevation gain 500 feet.**

The trail on the west side of Kanealole Stream is
usually wet and muddy, but it is a gentler ascent than
the Maunalaha Trail on the east side. The trail follows
an old road that was once used by work crews to control the growth in the valley. Although the hike is uphill, there is abundant shade along the trail, which
makes for a fairly cool and enjoyable hike for the
whole family. Look on the left side of the trail as you
ascend for surinam cherries (*Eugenia uniflora*) which,
when bright red, are quite sweet. This small, ovate
cherry from Brazil is a local favorite for making jelly.
At the junction with the Makiki Valley Trail, you can
follow it across the valley to the right or go left a
short distance and connect with the Nahuina Trail,
which will take you to Tantalus.

**Nahuina Trail, 0.6 mile one-way, ½ hour (trail rating:
hardy family). Elevation loss 600 feet.**

Nahuina was constructed by the Sierra Club's

Hawaii Chapter, which organized volunteers in 1979
to link the Tantalus and Makiki Valley hiking areas
(see map). The idea was good because there is a lot of
hiking pleasure to be gained from the loop hikes now
possible. From the Manoa Cliffs trailhead on Tantalus
Drive, the Nahuina Trail is easy to find. It is about
150 yards down the road on the left side (east), at the
end of a white guard rail. From the junction with the
Makiki Valley Trail, the Nahuina Trail heads north to
Tantalus Road.

Regardless of your point of departure, the first
part of the trail is in good condition. After a short
distance, fallen trees cross the trail and chest-high
vegetation completely covers it. (I suggest the Mokeka
Trail on the northeast side of the valley as a connecting trail between Tantalus-Round Top and Makiki
Valley.) If you take the Nahuina Trail, I urge caution
because it is usually muddy and slippery. On the
descent from Tantalus Drive, the trail is well-defined
for a short distance until a fallen, giant koa tree blocks
the trail. You can scramble uphill through or around
the tangle of roots and pick up the trail on the other
side. From here almost to the Makiki Valley Trail, be
alert and cautious because the trail is overgrown and
difficult to follow.

**Makiki Valley Trail, 1.1 miles one-way, 1 hour (trail
rating: family).**

This east-west trail traverses Makiki Valley. (The
valley was named after a type of stone found here
that was used as a weight for an octopus lure.) The
trailhead on the west side is about 2 miles up Tantalus
Drive from Makiki Heights Drive, north of a eucalyptus grove where the road makes a sharp turn. The
trailhead on the east side is about at the midpoint of
the Ualakaa Trail.

From the Tantalus Drive trailhead, the trail descends eastward through a forest into Makiki Valley,
passing the Nahuina Trail on the left (north) and,

shortly, the Kanealole Trail on the right (south). At this second junction, pause to look for springs in the brush to the left of the junction. The grass and brush should be matted where other hikers have made their way to the springs, 30 feet north of the junction. It is an enchanting place to pause to enjoy the beauty and the solitude. It is also a place to pick Job's tears (*Coix lacrymajobi*), which are abundant. The black, blue-gray and white, pea-sized beans of this plant are favorites with the local people, who string them into attractive necklaces, leis and rosaries. Ranging from one foot to six feet high, the plant is a coarse, branched grass with long, pointed leaves. The beans are easy for children to string with a needle and heavy thread.

From the junction, the trail turns in and out of small gulches and crosses a couple of small streams, passing through a richly foliated, forested valley. One of the many delights along this trail is the mountain apple (*Eugenia malaccensis*), which is abundant and within easy reach. What a treat! The apples are found on both sides of a stream in a very peaceful setting in which to pause and enjoy this succulent, red fruit. Up the hill from the stream at an unmarked junction, the Mokeka Trail goes to the left to meet the Manoa Cliffs Trail at Round Top Drive, the Makiki Valley Trail goes straight about ¼ mile more to end where it meets the Ualakaa Trail, and the Maunalaha Trail to the right goes to Makiki Valley and the baseyard.

Maunalaha Trail, 0.7 mile one-way, ½ hour (trail rating: family). Elevation loss 555 feet.

From the junction with the Makiki Valley Trail, the hike on the Maunalaha Trail is an easy downhill walk. The trail contours along Makiki Ridge, passing through avocado, juniper, eucalyptus and bamboo in the lower parts. Periodically, a break in the forest provides good views of Honolulu and of Manoa Valley to the east. One of the most interesting trees in the valley is the octopus, or umbrella, tree (*Brassaia actinophylla*), whose peculiar blossoms look like the long, spreading arms of an octopus. The new blossoms are first greenish-yellow, then light pink and finally deep red. As the trail levels, it crosses a footbridge over a stream, passes through the territorial nursery, and returns to the baseyard parking lot.

Moleka Trail, 0.5 mile, ½ hour one-way (trail rating: hardy family).

Joining the Makiki Valley and Tantalus-Round Top, the Moleka Trail, like the Nahuina, was constructed in 1979 by volunteers organized under the leadership of the Sierra Club's Hawaii Chapter. Of the two trails, the Moleka is in good condition and is easy to locate and to follow. The trailhead is on Round Top Drive opposite the Manoa Cliffs trailhead, southeast of the turnout and parking area.

Descending from Round Top Drive, you step into a natural garden of ti, ginger (both white and yellow), bamboo and the delightfully beautiful heliconia (*Heliconia humilis*), or "lobster claw," so named because the bright red bracts are similar to boiled lobster claws. The trail gently contours along the valley slope, providing numerous views into Makiki Valley. Be on the lookout for edible red thimbleberries along the trail, growing on a small thorny bush with white flowers. About midway, a side trail to the left (east) will take you to Round Top Drive. Continue down and to the right to reach a junction with the Makiki Valley Trail. From the junction, the Makiki Valley Trail goes to the left to join the Ualakaa Trail and to the right across Makiki Valley. The trail ahead, the Maunalaha Trail, descends to the Makiki Valley baseyard.

Ualakaa Trail, 0.6 mile one-way, ½ hour (trail rating: family).

The newest trail on Oahu, Ualakaa (lit., "rolling

sweet potato"), was constructed in 1980 by volunteers organized by the Sierra Club's Hawaii Chapter.
The purpose was to connect Puu Ualakaa State Park
with the Makiki/Tantalus hiking area.

The trailhead is 0.1 mile from the entrance of
Ualakaa State Park at telephone pole #9 on the right
side just as the road makes a sharp turn. From here,
the trail ascends, paralleling Round Top Drive for a
short distance until it meets, entering from the left,
the Makiki Valley Trail. The Ualakaa Trail ends
shortly on Round Top Drive just opposite Camp
Ehrhorn, a Boy Scout camp.

**Manoa Cliffs, 3 miles one-way, 2 hours (trail rating:
hardy family). Elevation gain 500 feet.**

Just 3 miles up Tantalus Drive, a sign identifying
the trail and a spur road that leads to a Hawaiian
Telephone Co. facility mark the trailhead for the
Manoa (lit., "vast") Cliffs Trail. The trail is well-
maintained and easy to follow. You are likely to
share the trail with students from the University of
Hawaii, since the area is used as an outdoor classroom.
The initial, forested part (1.2 miles) contours the hillside. A number of native and introduced plants, some
of which are identified by markers, are found along
the trail. According to the Division of Forestry, 33
native species of flora have been identified. You
should not have any trouble finding two introduced
plants whose fruit is edible. Guava (*Psidium guajava*)
trees are particularly abundant throughout the area.
The yellow, lemon-sized fruit is a tasty treat high in
Vitamin C.

About 1 mile from the trailhead, you reach a junction. The trail to the left (north) is well-defined and
will eventually join the Puu Ohia Trail at Pauoa Flats.
You may choose to continue on this unnamed trail
and to return to the Manoa Cliffs Trail via the Puu
Ohia Trail. At the junction with the unnamed trail,

the Manoa Cliffs Trail makes a sharp right and follows
switchbacks up a hill for 0.2 mile to the Manoa Cliffs/
Puu Ohia trails junction (actually, a pair of junctions
30 feet apart). Puu Ohia leads north (left) down the
hill and south (right) up the hill while the cliffs trail
continues east.

The remaining part of the Manoa Cliffs Trail hike
contours the hillside above Manoa Valley. Spectacu-
lar views of the valley are possible from a number of
viewpoints. Keep a sharp eye on small children, however, for parts of the hillside along the trail are steep.
There are a number of overgrown trails leading off
both sides of the trail which should be avoided. One
spur trail, a short distance east from the Manoa Cliffs/
Puu Ohia junction, switchbacks up the hill to meet
the Puu Ohia Trail. The Manoa Cliffs Trail turns south
and emerges on Round Top Drive at the other trailhead for this hike. Now it is 1.4 miles west (right) to
your car via the road or 0.9 mile west to the Puu Ohia
trailhead.

**Puu Ohia Trail, 2 miles one-way, 1½ hours (trail rat-
ing: hardy family). Elevation gain 500 feet.**

The Puu Ohia (lit., "ohia tree hill") trailhead is easy
to find. It is 0.5 mile from the Manoa Cliffs Trailhead
near the uppermost point of Round Top and Tantalus
drives, where you will find a large parking area opposite the trailhead (the nearest street number is 4050).
The first 0.5 mile of the trail follows a circuitous
route up a hill. The trail then straightens and goes
along the side of the ridge a short distance to where
a number of trails lead off down to the right. Bear
left and follow the trail to where it meets a paved
road, then follow the road to its end at a Hawaiian
Telephone Co. facility. The trail continues north from
behind and to the left of the telephone building and
descends to join the Manoa Cliffs Trail. As you de-
scend, bear to the left to avoid the somewhat over-

grown trails to the right and the one clear spur trail also on the right. This latter trail eventually meets the Manoa Cliffs Trail farther east. Soon you reach the Cliffs Trail, jog right 10 yards on it, and then continue north. The Puu Ohia Trail is wide but steep, so proceed with caution until you reach Pauoa Flats. Although the trail over the flats is level, it is usually wet and slippery and it has exposed roots which are potential ankle-busters.

Eucalyptus (*Eucalyptus robusta*) and paper-bark (*Melaleuca leucandendra*) trees dominate the flats area. The eucalyptus has thick, pointed leaves with a capsule type of fruit, while the distinguishing feature of the paper-bark tree is bark that can be peeled in sheets. This tree has been planted on the islands for conservation purposes in wet, boggy areas. There are a number of secondary trails on the flats where hikers have cut through the bamboo to vistas overlooking Manoa Valley, the Pali Highway, and Reservoir No. 4 in the Honolulu Watershed Forest Reserve. DO NOT hike beyond the lookout into the watershed area, which is protected by both law and good judgment.

MANOA FALLS

(Hiking Area No. 7)

Rating: Family.

Features: Waterfall, swimming, fruits.

Permission: None.

Hiking Distance & Time: .8 mile, 1 hour, 800-foot gain.

Driving Instructions: From Honolulu (3 miles, ¼ hour) drive north on Manoa Road past Paradise Park and Lyon Arboretum to the end of the road.

Bus Instructions: From Waikiki to Ala Moana Center take bus # 5 (Manoa/Ala Moana) to Paradise Park at the end of the line. Walk up the road to the trailhead.

Introductory Notes: The trail to Manoa (lit., "vast") Falls is easily accessible from downtown Honolulu, which probably accounts for its popularity. You can expect to share the trail and the pool with local people as well as visitors. Nevertheless, pack a lunch and make the trip to the falls, for it is worth the time. To reduce the risk of a break-in, park your car in the lot at Paradise Park and walk the short distance to the end of the road.

In 1978, under the leadership of the Sierra Club's Hawaii Chapter, volunteers constructed the Aihualama Trail, which connects Manoa Valley with the Makiki/Tantalus hiking area (No. 5). Now numerous hiking opportunities are open for the person who is looking for longer and more challenging hikes than the one to Manoa Falls. One suggestion for a delightful day's outing is to hike to Manoa Falls, follow Aihualama to Pauoa Flats, walk the Puu Ohia Trail to Manoa Cliffs, hike Moleka, and complete your trip in Makiki Valley or at Puu Ualakaa State Park.

On the Trail: A chain gate and a foot bridge at the end of the road mark the trailhead for the hike into Manoa Valley along Waihi (lit., "trickling water") Stream. Most of the trail is muddy and a bit slippery because heavy rains have washed away soil around trees and exposed their roots. The heavy rains also sustain a heavily foliated area where vegetation common to damp areas is abundant. The trail is easy to follow through the forest reserve. There are some fruit trees along the trail, but the likelihood of finding fruit is slim because of the popularity of the hike. The yellow, lemon-sized guava may be found as well as the popular mountain apple. This succulent apple is small and red, has a thin, waxy skin, and is usually ripe in June.

At midpoint, the canyon narrows and the footing becomes wetter. There are a number of larger pools where you may see hikers swimming or catching prawns, crayfish or frogs. The latter are particularly plentiful. You should be able to see the falls from a number of points along the trail. The junglelike setting at the falls makes for an enchanting place to swim and picnic if it is not too crowded.

The Division of Forestry prohibits entry into the closed watershed beyond the falls. Violators might damage a protected area and face the prospect of court appearances and fines. Furthermore, numerous injuries and a few fatalities have been recorded as a result of people hiking in this prohibited area.

Aihualama Trail, 1.4 miles, 1½ hours, 400-foot gain (trail rating: hardy family)

Do not mistake the precipitous and dangerous trail to the left of Manoa Falls for Aihualama. Beginning 50 feet from the falls, the Aihualama Trail follows a gentle zigzag path to Pauoa Flats. Enjoy the views provided along the first part of the trail. After 150 yards, turn for a good view of upper and lower Manoa Falls and across Manoa Valley to Waahila Ridge on the east side. A bit farther on, a view of the tip of Diamond Head and Waikiki is possible. The trail can be wet and muddy due to frequent showers throughout the year, but the rewards are great. Huge koa (*Acacia koa*) trees, with their crescent-shaped leaves, and interesting banyan (*Ficus benghalensis*) trees, with their aerial roots growing earthward from horizontal branches, combine with aromatic and delightfully beautiful ginger to excite the hiker.

After following the contour of the hill, the trail begins to switchback. Just before reaching Pauoa Flats, the trail cuts through a bamboo forest, which offers some interesting sights and sounds as the wind passes over the flatland and through the bamboo. At an unmarked junction, the Pauoa Flats trail turns right, and at the end of that trail, about .5 mile distant, there are views of Nuuanu Valley. The trail to the left goes to the Puu Ohia/Manoa Cliffs trail junction.

Manoa Falls

WAAHILA RIDGE

(Hiking Area No. 8)

Rating: Hardy family.

Features: Views of Honolulu and Manoa Valley, fruits, native and introduced flora.

Permission: None.

Hiking Distance & Time: 2 miles, 2 hours, 700-foot gain.

Driving Instructions: From Honolulu (4 miles, ¼ hour) drive north up St. Louis Drive, turn left on

Peter St., and then left on Ruth Place to the entrance to Waahila State Park. Drive to the upper
end of the park.

Bus Instructions: From Waikiki take bus #14 (St.
Louis Heights) to the end of the line at Peter
Street/Ruth Place. Walk up Ruth Place to Waahila
Ridge State Park and to the trailhead.

Introductory Notes: Waahila Ridge State Park is a
good place close to Honolulu to picnic, to enjoy
a cool, forested park, and to share a hike with the
family.

On the Trail: Proceed northeast from the parking
area on a dirt road which is used to service the power-
transmission lines on the ridge. A number of paths
lead off the road into the guava trees, which are
plentiful, but the yellow, lemon-sized fruit may be
difficult to find because park visitors pick it as fast
as it ripens. At 0.4 mile, a trail goes left and then
shortly rejoins the road, which has by now narrowed
to a trail. The two trails meet under a cluster of poles
on top of the ridge. From under this network of
transmission lines, the trail follows the narrow
Waahila (the name of a female chief who excelled in a
dance named for her) Ridge, which separates Manoa
and Palolo (lit., "clay") valleys. The Norfolk Island
pines and other exotics bordering the trail were planted about 40 years ago in an effort to improve the
watershed and the esthetic and recreational value of
the ridge area. The trail makes a few steep descents
and ascents along the ridge, which require some caution, particularly if wet and muddy. The frequent
views of Manoa Valley and Honolulu through the
dense forest are striking. The majestic koa *(Acacia
koa)* tree can be seen in the valley and on the ridge. A
native of Hawaii, and frequently called Hawaiian
mahogany, the koa had a wide range of uses by
Hawaiians. It was prized for making canoes, and was

also used to make surfboards, cálabashes, ukuleles,
and a variety of household furniture. Growing to
heights of 100 feet, the koa has a large trunk and
crescent-shaped leaves.

At a junction at the 2-mile point you must turn
around unless you wish to take the steeply descending trail on the left, which emerges on Alani Drive in
Manoa Valley. To reach downtown Honolulu from
the end of this trail, continue south on Alani Drive,
right on East Manoa Road, and left on Oahu Ave.,
which becomes University Ave. just before reaching
the campus of the University of Hawaii. You may
choose to follow this trail if you do not have to return to the park for your vehicle.

Hiking from the junction on the trail to the summit of the Koolau Mountains is prohibited by law,
since the ridge continues into the Honolulu Watershed Forest Reserve. There are other trails to the
summit of the Koolau Range described in this book
(Lanipo—Hiking Area No. 9—for example) which are
legal to hike. The view from Lanipo is equal to that
at the end of Waahila Ridge.

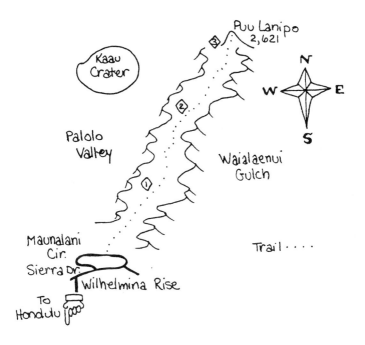

LANIPO

(Hiking Area No. 9)

Rating: Strenuous.

Features: View from Koolau Mountain Range, native and introduced flora.

Permission: None.

Hiking Distance & Time: 3 miles, 3 hours, 1,600-foot gain.

Driving Instructions: From Honolulu (6 miles, ½ hour) drive southeast on H-1 to Koko Head turn-off. Go left over freeway toward mountains, then right on Waialae Ave., and then take the first left, Wilhelmina Rise, to the top of the hill and 4969 Maunalani Circle, where a public-access passageway begins on the left of the driveway between fences."

Bus Instructions: From Waikiki at Kalakaua/Kapahulu
Ave. take bus #14 (Maunalani Heights) to Sierra
Drive/Lurline Drive. Walk up Sierra Drive to Mau-
nalani Circle and to the trailhead.

Introductory Notes: The Lanipo and Wiliwilinui (Hiking Area No. 10) trails are parallel hikes to peaks
along the Koolau Mountain Range. Indeed, an experienced and daring hiker could join the trails by hiking
½ mile along an extremely precipitous and dangerous
ridge on the Koolau Range. Do not attempt this connecting hike alone. In any event, both hikes, while
strenuous, are worth the effort, for the views from
the summit of the east side of the island are stunning.
Of the two, I prefer Lanipo because it is a 3-mile
foot trail whereas the first 2½ miles of Wiliwilinui are
on a jeep road. The Lanipo trail also skirts Kaau
Crater.

On the Trail: The trail initially ascends along a fenced
walkway for about 100 yards, to a point on Mauumae
(lit., "wilted grass") Ridge. After a short descent, the
trail traverses a number of saddles along the ridge.
The first two saddles are a bit steep, with loose rock
underfoot, so that caution is advised to avoid sore
feet or a twisted ankle. The flora along the ridge is
mostly low scrub and low trees, so that views of the
surrounding area are unobstructed. To the west (left)
Palolo (lit., "clay") Valley extends north to Kaau
(lit., "forty") Crater which lies at the base of the
Koolau Range ridge. The ¼-mile-wide crater, legend
holds, was formed by the demigod Maui who, want-
ing to join Kauai and Oahu, threw out a great hook
hoping to catch the foundation of Kauai. He gave a
tremendous tug and loosed a rock. The rock fell at his
feet where he was standing at Kaena Point on Oahu,
while his hook sailed over his head and landed in
Palolo Valley, creating Kaau Crater.

After the midpoint of the hike, the ridge narrows considerably. Thereafter, the trail is wet, muddy and steep, and it is necessary to grasp branches and roots of plants to continue. However, there are level places to rest and to enjoy a panorama of Diamond Head and the Honolulu area.

A variety of native plants can be identified. Look for the following: ulei (*Osteomeles anthyllidifolia*), a single, sweet-scented, thornless Hawaiian rose; kawau (*Byronia sandwicensis*) a Hawaiian holly tree with white blossoms and black berries; and the common yet beautiful and interesting ohia lehua (*Metrosideros collina*), a plant that varies in size from a shrub to a tree 100 feet tall. The leaves are usually small, rounded or blunt, and grayish, and the flower appears as a tuft of red stamens emerging from close-growing petals. Visitors frequently identify it as a bottlebrush tree due to the close similarity of the two. Both the lehua and the bottlebrush are in the myrtle family. Legend says that the lehua is a favorite of Pele, goddess of volcanoes, who will cause rain unless an offering is made before a lehua flower is picked.

The last ½ mile is steep and requires agility to climb the precipitous ridge, to make your way around thick brush, and to avoid mud holes. But the views from the summit are ample reward for your efforts. You have a sweeping view of the east side, from the town of Waimanalo (lit., "potable water") to the northeast, to Kailua (lit., "two seas") to the north, and along the magnificent Koolau Range extending west. All this, and a plentiful supply of thimbleberries, await the hiker at the summit. Puu Lanipo (lit., "dense peak") (2621 feet elevation) is to the east (right), on the way to the Wiliwilinui Trail.

WILIWILINUI

(Hiking Area No. 10)

Rating: Strenuous.

Features: Views from the Koolau Mountain Range, native flora and fauna.

Permission: None.

Hiking Distance & Time: 3 miles, 3 hours, 2000-foot gain.

Driving Instructions: From Honolulu (10 miles, ½ hour) drive southeast on H-1, which becomes Route 72. Turn left on Laukahi Street (0.6 mile from the end of the freeway) and drive to the top of the road, to an unpaved road which marks the trailhead. (Ongoing housing construction has advanced the trailhead farther up the ridge.)

Bus Instructions: From Waikiki take bus #58 (Sea Life
Park) to Kahala Mall and transfer to bus #21
(Laukahi Shuttle) to the end of the line and walk up
Laukahi Street to the trailhead.

On the Trail: From the top of the paved road and
beyond the private housing, you should be able to locate
an unpaved road that extends 2 miles up Wiliwilinui (lit.,
"large wiliwili"—a native tree bearing red seeds) Ridge
overlooking Kapakahi (lit., "crooked") Gulch to the west
and Wailupe (lit., "kite water") Gulch to the east. Shortly
beyond the trailhead look on the left and right sides of
the trail for abandoned WW II gun emplacements, which
are partly hidden by brush. They are large, and fun to
explore.

You should see numerous birds along the trail. The
elpaio (*Chasiempis sanwichensis*), an endemic bird that is
common throughout the forest, has a gray back, a rather
long, blackish tail and a white rump. It is a somewhat
noisy and curious bird, giving forth with what is best
described as a sort of "wolf whistle." Another native
bird, the apapane (*Himatione sanguinea*), can be found
feeding on the nectar of the ohia flowers. It is a deep-
crimson bird with black wings and tail and a slightly
curved black bill.

In spite of the 2000-foot elevation gain to the summit, the route along the road is a relatively gentle
ascent, but it can be muddy and wet by the time you
reach the foot trail. lantana (*Lantana camara*) is a
common flower that blossoms almost continuously in
the surrounding forest. Its flowers vary in color from
yellow to orange to pink to red. Another common
yet delicate and pretty flower is the wild, or Philip-
pine, orchid (*Spathoglottis plicata*). Usually lavender,
it has what appear to be five starlike petals but are
actually two petals and three sepals.

The road ends at about 1800 feet elevation and the
foot trail extends to the summit, ½ mile and an 800-

foot elevation gain distant. The trail ascends mostly under newly constructed telephone lines and past telephone installations. The climb on the foot trail is usually wet and muddy and somewhat treacherous. The view of the east side is magnificent, from Waimanalo to the east to Kualoa (lit., "long back") Point to the north-northwest. The trail to Lanipo goes west along the pali, if you dare to take it.

Hanauma Bay from Koko Crater

HANAUMA BAY

(Hiking Area No. 11)

Rating: See individual hikes.

Features: Swimming, snorkeling, tidepools, historical sites, blowhole, views of coastal area.

Permission: None.

Hiking Distance & Time: See individual hikes.

Driving Instructions: From Honolulu (12 miles, ½ hour) drive southeast on H-1, which becomes Route 72, then right on Hanauma Bay Road to parking lot.

Bus Instructions: From Waikiki at Kalakaua/Monsarat streets, take bus #22 (Beach Bus—daily in summer; only weekends in nonsummer months) to Hanauma Bay. Otherwise, take bus #58 (Sea Life Park) to Lunalilo Home Road and walk up the hill to a parking area and then down a trail to the bay.

Introductory Notes: To visit Oahu but fail to hike and swim at Hanauma is a mistake. Hanamua Bay is not only a strikingly beautiful place, but it also offers a variety of hiking experiences.

On the Trail: Koko Head Trail, 1 mile, ½ hour, 450-foot gain (trail rating: family)

For the protection of your vehicle and for convenience, park in the parking lot at the end of the bay road overlooking Hanauma Bay. To reach the trailhead, walk up the bay road to the highway (Route 72). A gate across a paved road on the left (west) prevents vehicular travel to the summit of Koko (lit., "blood") Head. Climb through the gate or walk around it for the short hike to the summit. Enchanting views of Hanauma (lit., "curved bay" or "hand-wrestling bay") Bay and a panorama of the surrounding area are had along the road. Koko Head is a 642-foot-high tuff cone and, according to legend, is the last place on Oahu that Pele, the goddess of vol-

To Waimanalo

Blowhole

Koko Crater

Summit 1,208'

Trail.....

Toilet Bowl

Hanauma Bay

N E S W

Ocean

Nonoula

Iheihelauakea

72

To Honolulu

Koko Head 642'

canoes, attempted to make a home for herself. From the summit, there are good views west to Diamond Head, north to the Koolau Mountain Range and Hawaii Kai (Henry Kaiser's 6000-acre town development) and northeast to Koko Crater and the coastline around Hanauma. Two small craters are below the summit to the east: Nonoula (lit., "red sunburned") on the left and Iheihelauakea (lit., "wide-leafed ihiihi"—an extinct or unknown plant that may have grown here) on the right. Look directly east and, if it is clear, you should see the island of Molokai some 20 miles across the channel. If you decide to return to the bay by crossing the two craters below, proceed with caution. There is no trail, and the slopes on the bay side of the craters are precipitous and dangerous.

Koko Crater, 1 mile, 1 hour, 1000-foot gain (trail rating: strenuous)

To reach the trailhead from Hanauma Bay, return to the main highway (Route 72). Take the road opposite the bay road by the sign identifying the "Aloha Hawaii Job Corps Training Center." It is ½ mile to the main office, behind which you will find an abandoned inclined railroad which leads directly to the summit.

The railroad ties make a convenient stepped path. Portions of the track are overgrown, so you can expect to have your arms and legs scratched by the brush. Be cautious when you cross over a gulch on a trestle about halfway to the summit. You should also be cautious when walking on the steps and platforms of the abandoned station on the summit, because the wood is broken and rotted in many places. The views from the old powerhouse and the 1208-foot lookout offer a 360° panorama. The Koolau Mountain Range to the north, Diamond Head and Hawaii Kai to the west, Koko Head and Hanauma Bay to the south, and the shoreline to the east treat the eye and calm the

spirit after a hard climb. The crater, 1000 feet below,
contains a botanical garden and bridle trails. Kohe-
lepelepe (lit., "fringed vagina") was the old name for
the crater.

**Hanauma Bay to Blowhole, 2 miles, 1½ hours (trail
rating: hardy family)**

In 1967 Hanauma Bay was declared a marine-life
conservation district, which meant that no marine life
could be caught here or injured in any manner. Consequently, it is a delightful experience to investigate
tidepools or to snorkel and to observe the variety of
sea life underwater. Hanauma Bay was once a crater,
until the sea broke through the southeast crater wall.

From the beach, hike along the shelf above the
water on the east side of the bay. Be alert not only
for interesting tidepools but also for waves which
may splash onto the shelf. While the danger of being
overcome by a wave is slight, it is wise to keep a
watchful eye on the water. Be certain to visit the
popular "toilet bowl" just beyond the far end of the
bay. This interesting feature is a hole about 30 feet
in circumference and 10 feet deep which is alternately filled and emptied from beneath as waves come in
and recede. Bathers jump or slide into the bowl as
it fills. Then, to escape, they scramble out when the
water rises to the top of the bowl. Try it. It's different!

From the "toilet bowl" you can climb to the ridge
overlooking the bay or follow the coastline around
Palea (lit., "brushed aside") Point. From here to the
blowhole you are likely to find many local people
fishing and snorkeling, so pause to examine their
catches and to exchange pleasantries. You will find
that a smile and an inquisitive attitude will usually
make a friend.

After the first mile, you may choose to hike to the
road and to follow it to the blowhole, since the ledge
above the water is narrow, and one needs some agility

to climb, crawl and jump over the lava while trying to avoid the crashing surf. However, by timing the waves and by using good judgment, you can make it to the blowhole at Halona (lit., "peering place") Point. A blowhole is a narrow vent in the lava through which water is forced by the charging surf. The blowhole at Halona Point "blows" water geysers 30-50 feet into the air, depending on surf conditions. It is a happy terminus to a delightful hike.

To Hauula

Kahana Bay

To Honolulu

83

Visitor Center

Kahana Valley Tr. (4.5)

Pavilion

Kahana Wells I

N
W — E
S

Dam

Hunting Area

Trail · · · ·
Trail Mileage ( )

Kahana Stream

KAHANA VALLEY

(Hiking Area No. 11)

Rating: Hardy family.

Features: Mountain apples, rose apple, swimming, "living park."

Permission: Division of State Parks, 1151 Punchbowl St., Room 310, Honolulu, Hawaii, 96813 (Phone 548-7455).

Hiking Distance & Time: 4.5 miles, 2½ hours.

Driving Instructions: From Honolulu (26 miles, 1 hour) drive northwest on H-1, then right on Route 61 (Pali Highway), then left on Route 83 to Kahana Valley State Park.

Bus Instructions: From Ala Moana Center take bus #55 (Kaneoha/Circle Island) to Kahana Valley State Park.

Introductory Notes: Kahana (lit., "cutting") Valley State Park has been designated by the state legislature as a "living park." By definition, such a park is intended "to nurture and foster native Hawaiian culture and spread knowledge of its values and ways, and that in such a living park the individuals living there shall participate in the purposes of the park by helping in the education of the public and by incorporating into the structure of their daily lives such values and ways."

In July 1980 a committee composed of state-park officials and valley residents was formed to develop a program which will be offered to visitors. In the late summer of that year, the state completed a visitor center and a pavilion where some of the 140 valley residents and others will exhibit their skills so that visitors may learn about the traditional Hawaiian way of life in Kahana Valley.

Kahana was once a thriving self-contained community where the people practiced the traditional concept of "ohana"—family units related by blood, marriage and adoption. Ample annual rainfall (average of 75 inches along the coast to 300 inches in the back of the valley) sustained the farms, and the ocean provided seafood for the residents. To date, the Bishop Museum has identified 120 small wet terraces and 12 irrigation canals constructed to grow taro, from which the Hawaiian staple food poi was produced.

The Kahana Valley hike is an enjoyable walk for the entire family. Be certain to secure a hiking permit because it will be checked by a caretaker.

On the Trail: From the visitor center, a jeep road leads into the valley for a little over a mile, to a fourth and last gate and the beginning of a hunting area and of a loop trail into the valley. Along this first mile, you pass some residences and then a couple of demonstration pavilions and public restrooms. Shortly, you pass the "Kahana Well" facility on the right, then a couple of hunter checking stations, and, just before the beginning of the loop trail, a papaya grove.

At the last gate, a large sign on the right side inside the gate identifies the entrance to the hunting area. From this junction one jeep road goes left for a couple of hundred yards and ends at the stream and a dam. The road to the right, bordered by hala trees, ends in about ¼ mile and a foot trail continues into the valley. After crossing a small stream, the first part of the foot trail passes through a mountain-apple orchard. In season—usually between June and August here—these succulent red apples are the highlight of the trip.

Beyond a second small stream crossing, the loop trail is pleasant and easy to follow until it nears Kahana Stream. Just before the stream, a number of spur trails go in different directions. The loop trail (taped in 1986) bears to the left and descends to Kahana Stream. The trail (taped) to the right leads through thick foliage about 0.5 mile to a stream and a marvelous swimming hole. Rose apple (*Eugenia jambos*), an edible, egg-shaped golden fruit with rose-water taste and odor is plentiful here. Related to the mountain apple, the rose-apple tree is an evergreen with narrow, pointed leaves and large, greenish-white pompon flowers. At the stream, you should be opposite a concrete water intake that is under a tangle of branches of a hau tree. Cross the stream here and crawl under the limbs to the trail, which becomes clear a short distance beyond the hau trees. The trail ascends out of this small gulch for 0.2 mile to where it makes a sharp left and descends ½ mile to the stream and the dam.

Because of the heavy rainfall in the valley, it is not always easy to make the stream crossing. If you make it, be alert for the trail-marking tape on trees, which will direct you to the dam, the gauging station and the swimming holes. If the water is too high, you may retrace your steps to the junction at the last gate and from there follow the jeep road east to the dam.

PUU PIEI

(Hiking Area No. 12)

Rating: Strenuous.

Features: Views of Kahana Bay and the nearby coast-line.

Permission: None.

Hiking Distance & Time: .8 mile, 1 hour, 1700-foot gain.

Driving Instructions: From Honolulu (26 miles, 1 hour) drive northwest on H-1, then right on Route 61 (Pali Highway), then left on Route 83 to Kahana Bay Beach Park. Park north of the restrooms.

Bus Instructions: From Ala Moana Center take bus #55 (Kaneohe/Circle Island) to Kahana Beach Park. Walk to the trailhead north of the restrooms.

Introductory Notes: Do not try this hike unless you are a confident hiker. The climb to the summit, though short, is extremely steep and the footing is mostly loose volcanic rock.

On the Trail: Across the road from the boat launching ramp between telephone poles #313 and #314, hala (*Pandanus tectorius*) trees mark the trailhead for the "assault" on Puu Piei (probably, "to peer hill"). Hala is an indigenous tree that grows in coastal areas. It is sometimes called "tourist pineapple," since the fruit resembles a pineapple and is jokingly identified as such by locals for tourists. It has been and continues to be a valuable resource. The hollow trunk of the female tree has been used as a pipe for drainage between taro patches, and the leaves have been used for weaving many items, such as baskets, mats and hats—hats being particularly popular with tourists.

After crossing the drainage ditch, bear left and follow the ridgeline on both sides of which the octopus tree abounds. The trail is in poor condition and is eroded by heavy rains in places so much that you may not wish to ascend to the end of the trail, for it climbs the narrow and precipitous ridge to the summit. There is a cable along the ridgeline to assist hikers, but be sure to test it, since it may not be reliable. The view from the summit makes the hike worth the effort. To the east, lovely Kahana (lit., "cutting") Bay lies at your feet and the panorama of the coast is extraordinary.

Kahana Bay from Puu Piei Trail

SACRED FALLS

(Hiking Area No. 13)

Rating: Hardy family.

Features: Waterfall, swimming, fruits.

Permission: None.

Hiking Distance & Time: 2.2 miles, 1½ hours.

Driving Instructions: From Honolulu (23 miles, 1¼ hours) drive northwest on H-1, turn right on Route 61 (Pali Highway), then left on Route 83 to the sign "Sacred Falls State Park" on the left.

Bus Instructions: From Ala Moana Center take bus #55 (Kaneohe/Circle Island) to Sacred Falls State Park.

Introductory Notes: Until recently the hike to Sacred Falls was commercialized, and a fee was charged to park at the end of the cane road. Kaliuwaa (lit., "canoe hold" or "canoe leak") is the Hawaiian name for Sacred Falls. Probably the name was changed because "Kaliuwaa" is difficult to pronounce and because "Sacred Falls" sounds more romantic to most tourists. In truth, ancient Hawaiian belief regards the entire valley as sacred to the gods. Legend holds that the pool at the base of the falls is bottomless and leads to another world where a demon lives. The waves in the pool are thought to represent the struggle between the demon and the thrust of the falls, which prevents him from entering this world. Interestingly, another Hawaiian name for the falls and pool is Kaluanua, which literally means "the big pit." To pacify the gods thought to live in the area, believers wrap a stone in a ti leaf and place it along the trail. They believe this act will protect them from falling rocks. Don't miss this hike. Although the trail is usually muddy, it is a fairly easy stroll for the family and offers fruits, picnicking and swimming.

On the Trail: From the trailhead it is 1.2 miles on a cane road to the valley trail. Ahead, you can see the narrow canyon that contains the falls. The road terminates at a large, flat, grassy area that once served as a parking lot. On the left side of this open place, the road becomes a trail, which then crosses a dry stream bed and ascends gently into the canyon. Shortly, the trail reaches Kaluanua Stream, where it is necessary to rock-hop or wade. Beyond the stream, you will find countless mountain-apple trees bearing small, delicious red apples in season.

In addition to the legends mentioned above, this enchanting, lush island paradise is said to be the home of Kamapuaa (lit., "child of a hog"), who was half human and half swine. Near the end of the valley to the left of the trail, you will cross at the base of a dry fall. This is the site, legend recounts, where Kamapuaa turned himself into a giant hog so that his followers could escape a pursuing army by climbing up his back to safety on the ledge above. The deep impression where water only occasionally falls is said to have been made by the weight and size of his body. At this point you might choose to wrap a rock in a ti leaf and place it on the rock fall: no reason to take any chance of being hit by falling rocks, since the valley soon narrows to a 50-feet width.

The falls can be heard crashing to the valley floor and can be seen around the next turn in the trail after a stream crossing. The valley walls rise to 1600 feet, but the falls drop only 87 feet. The generous pool at the base is usually muddy and very cold. You might wish to swim or splash in the stream just below the pool. In any event, there is plenty of room for a picnic on the large rocks in this cool, shaded canyon.

Sacred Falls

HAUULA

(Hiking Area No. 14)

Rating: See individual hikes.

Features: Views of valley and coastal areas, swimming, waterfall, fruits, native and introduced flora.

Permission: None.

Hiking Distance & Time: See individual hikes.

Driving Instructions: From Honolulu (30 miles, 1¼ hours) drive northwest on H-1, right on Route 61 (Pali Highway), left on Route 83 to Hauula, left on Hauula Homestead Road opposite the north end of Hauula Beach Park for .2 mile and park at the intersection with Maakua Road.

Bus Instructions: From Ala Moana Center take bus #55 (Kaneohe/Circle Island) to Hauula Beach Park. Cross the highway and walk up Hauula Homestead Road to the trailhead.

Introductory Notes: Three relatively easy hikes, camping and swimming await the outdoorsperson in this 20th century Hawaiian community. In Hauula (lit., "abundant hau") you will find old Hawaii mixed with the new. You will find local people surf fishing, throwing a net, "talking stories" and having 3-4 generation ohana ("family") picnics on the beach. There are not many tourists who hike these trails, but you are likely to encounter local school children with their teacher or Boy Scouts with their leader.

On the Trail: Hauula, 2.5 miles loop, 1½ hours, 600-foot gain (trail rating: hardy family)

Walk straight between the houses on Maakua Road to a clearing where the pavement ends. Continue on the dirt road for 100 yards, then bear left for another 100 yards to where the dirt road becomes mere trail, and 100 yards farther, at a junction, the Maakua Gulch Trail veers left while the less-trod Hauula Trail goes straight ahead. A jeep road turns off to the right shortly before the junction. You pass through some heavy brush, ford a small stream and then switchback up a ridge to where Norfolk Island pines dominate. The fallen needles provide a soft underfooting and make the air aromatic. At midpoint along the ridge, do not take the trail entering on the right but bear left up the ridge. The trail switchbacks up the ridge, traverses Waipilopilo (lit., "smelly water") Gulch, and then ascends along another ridge overlooking Kaipapau (lit., "shallow sea") Valley, from which you have good views of the Koolau Mountain Range and of the east-side coastline and of Hauula. The route then gently slopes and descends to join the initial portion of the trail, on which you retrace your steps.

Maakua Gulch, 3 miles, 3 hours, 1,100-foot gain (trail rating: strenuous)

Walk straight between the houses on Maakua Road to a clearing where the pavement ends. Continue on the dirt road for 100 yards, then bear left for another 100 yards to where the dirt road becomes mere trail, and 100 yards farther, at a junction, the Maakua Gulch Trail veers left while the less-trod Hauula Trail goes straight ahead. Just 140 yards farther, you pass the start of the Papali Trail on the left.

Maakua Gulch becomes narrower and narrower, and the trail twists and turns along a route which crisscrosses the stream countless times. Be prepared to get wet and to rock-hop throughout the last half of the hike, since the trail is in the streambed there. The narrow canyon and its high, steep walls make this an enchanting hike. Another compensation is the frequent clusters of red mountain apple trees and a good supply of guava trees. The beautiful kukui (*Aleurites moluccana*) tree is common in the gulch. Nicknamed the "candlenut tree," the kukui tree was a valuable resource until the 20th century. Kukui-nut oil was burned for light, the trunk was used to make canoes if the more durable koa tree was not available, and beautiful and popular leis were made of the nuts. To make a lei, each nut must be sanded, filed and polished to a brilliant luster that is acquired from its own oil. Kukui is also the Hawaii State tree. The hike ends at the base of a small cascade—or, if you're an expert scrambler, the base of a small waterfall just above. At the bottom of the waterfall and the bottom of the cascade are pools large enough for a cooling dip.

Papali, 2.5 mile loop, 2 hours, 800-foot gain (trail rating: hardy family)

Walk straight between the houses on Maakua Road to a clearing where the pavement ends. Continue on the dirt road for 100 yards, then bear left for another 100 yards to where the dirt road becomes mere trail, and 100 yards farther, at a junction, the less-trod Hauula Trail goes straight ahead but your trail veers left. Just 140 yards past the junction, on the left, is the overgrown start of the Papali (lit., "small cliff or slope") Trail. You have to duck and bend to get through the hau (*Hibiscus tiliaceus*) trees at the trailhead. In the wild, this yellow-flowered hibiscus grows twisting and branching along the ground, forming an impenetrable mass of tangled branches. The lightweight hau wood was used for canoe outriggers, fish floats, adze handles and fence posts. Maakua Stream slowly trickles through the hau grove and must be crossed. The trail then climbs sharply along switchbacks, passing concrete slabs that once supported water tanks. The trail heads toward the mountains for about a mile and then turns east and descends into Papali Gulch and crosses tiny Papali Stream. Although you'll share the scenic stream crossing with mosquitoes, pause in this serene place. Civilization seems a long way off. From here, the trail ascends along the ridge, until it rejoins the earlier trail segment near the concrete slabs. In the last mile of the hike you have outstanding views of Hauula town and north to Laie (lit., "'ie leaf") Point.

LAIE

(Hiking Area No. 15)

Rating: Strenuous.

Features: Views of east and west sides of the island, native flora, fruits, swimming.

Permission: Secure hiking permit from Zions Securities Corp.

Hiking Distance & Time: 3 miles, 3 hours, 1400-foot gain.

Driving Instructions: From Honolulu (36 miles, 1½ hours) drive northwest on H-1, right on Route 61 (Pali Highway), left on Route 83 to Laie. Go left on Naniloa Loop Road just past the Laie Shopping Center, bear right on Poohaili Road, which shortly becomes a cane road. Drive 1 mile to a chain gate and park here; the road beyond is not passable in a conventional car.

Bus Instructions: From Ala Moana Center take bus #55 (Kaneoha/Circle Island) to the Laie Shopping Center. Walk north on the highway, left on Naniloa Loop Road, bear right on Poohaili Street, and follow the cane road to the trailhead.

Introductory Notes: Laie attracts thousands of tourists yearly—not to hike in its charming valley, but to visit the Polynesian Cultural Center. A Morman settlement built over 100 years ago, Laie has, in addition to the cultural center that is owned and operated by the Mormon Church, a branch campus of Brigham Young University and the "Taj Mahal of the Pacific"—the Morman Temple.

On the Trail: From the chain gate follow the jeep road 1 mile up the ridge, bearing to the left at an abandoned dumping ground to a grove of Norfolk Island Pines. The trail begins on the mountain side of the grove and contours the side of the main ridge. Strawberry guavas, abundant along the first part of the trail, are a treat to supplement your lunch. This red, walnut-sized fruit can be eaten whole or after removing the small seeds inside. After the first mile, look for a spur trail west (right) which leads into Kahawainui (lit., "great stream") Gulch and along Kahawainui Stream, where a small waterfall and a pool await the hiker.

The main trail continues on the ridge and is well-defined for the next mile, after which it is heavily overgrown and difficult to follow to the summit at 2200 feet. Unless the weather is clear, there is little point in continuing since it is usually windy and cold at the top. But when clear, your view extends west to Mokuleia and the Waianae Mountain Range. A small, open, flat area marks the summit, from which several foot trails lead to viewpoints. CAUTION: If you follow any of these trails, be certain to mark your path, particularly in cloudy weather.

AIEA LOOP

(Hiking Area No. 16)

Rating: Hardy family.

Features: Views of Pearl Harbor, fruits, camping, Keaiwa Heiau.

Permission: Camping permits from Division of State Park.

Hiking Distance & Time: 4.8 miles, 3-hour loop.

Driving Instructions: From Honolulu (12 miles, ½ hour) drive northwest on H-1, bear left at sign "Aiea #78," go right at "Aiea" turnoff and follow Moanalua Road downhill to a right turn on Aiea Heights Drive, and go to its end. After entering the park, follow the one-way road to the northeast end of the park and a sign marking the upper Aiea Loop trailhead.

Bus Instructions: From Ala Moana Center take bus #11 (Aiea Heights) to Aiea and to the Kaamilo/Aiea

Heights Drive junction. Walk up Aiea Heights Drive
to Keaiwa Heiau State Park and to the trailhead.

Introductory Notes: Take time to visit the remains of
the heiau (a pre-Christian place of worship) by the
park entrance. Keaiwa (lit., "the mystery") Heiau was
an ancient healing temple where a priest by the same
name was said to have had mysterious healing powers.
Keaiwa used the plants grown in the area for medicin-
al purposes, and instructed novitiates in the art of
healing. As is true at so many heiaus in the Islands,
little remains of the structures, since they were made
mainly of wood and grass. Nevertheless, interpretive
displays here provide some information.

Kaeiwa Heiau State Park offers a good family
hiking trail, first-class picnic grounds in the forested
setting, and a comfortable campground. The Aiea
(lit., "Nothocestrum tree") Loop Trail is likely to be

On the Aiea Loop Trail

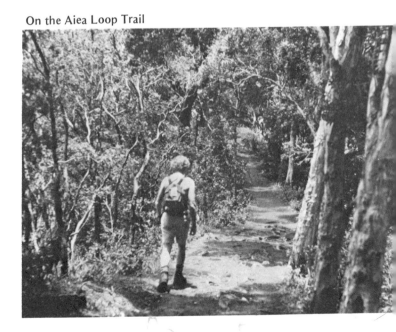

crowded on weekends, when local people come to
enjoy the park and to hike.

On the Trail: The first part of the trail snakes along
the ridge on a wide and well-maintained path where
you can identify thin-barked eucalyptus, symmetrical
Norfolk Island pine and ironwood (*Casuarina equise-
tifolia*), with its long, thin, drooping, dull green
needles. Many of these trees are the result of a refor-
estation program begun by Thomas McGuire in 1928.
The shade from the big trees and the trade winds
make this part of the hike both cool and pleasurable.
Guava is abundant, and with luck you may find ripe
strawberry guava, a red, walnut-sized fruit.

The trail makes a sharp right turn at 1.6 miles,
where a trail to Koolau Ridge departs eastward, and
then follows the ridge above North Halawa (lit.,
"curve") Stream, from which views of the Koolau
Mountains and North Halawa Valley are good. The
trail descends through a forest of trees, where you
will find some native trees, including koa and ohia
lehua. At the 3-mile point, look to the right of the
trail for the remains of a C-47 cargo plane that crash-
ed in 1943. Just beyond the crash site, a bridle path
leads off to the left to Camp Smith and then the loop
trail swings to the right and downhill to cross Aiea
Stream. Before crossing the stream, you may choose
to stroll along a trail to the left which follows the
stream. The Aiea Loop trail crosses the stream and
then climbs up to the campground and the lower
Aiea Loop trailhead, which is just across the grass
below the only toilet building in the camping area.

WAIMANO

(Hiking Area No. 17)

Rating: Difficult.

Features: Views from the Koolau Mountain Range, swimming, native and introduced flora.

Permission: None.

Hiking Distance & Time: 7.1 miles, 4 hours, 1600-foot gain.

Driving Instructions: From Honolulu (14 miles, ½ hour) drive northwest on H-1 to Pearl City (Exit 10) bear right on Moanalua Road to its end, then right on Waimano Home Road (1.7 miles) to the end at a guard shelter. The trailhead is on the left side of the fence at a trail register.

Bus Instructions: From Ala Moana Center take bus #53 (Pacific Palisades) to Pearl City Shopping Center (Kamehameha Highway and Waimano Home Road intersection). Transfer to Pearlridge-Pearl City shuttle bus and take to Komo Mai Drive. Walk up Waimano Home Road to the trailhead.

Introductory Notes: Waimano (lit., "many waters") is one of a number of hikes in this book which take the hiker to viewpoints overlooking the east side of the island from the Koolau Mountain Range. Although this is a much longer hike than the others, there are places to swim and to splash in Waimano Stream. Otherwise the forested area is similar to the other hikes (Hiking Area Nos. 18, 19 and 21).

On the Trail: The trail parallels the fence a short distance and then descends for about ¼ mile to the stream. An abandoned, rusting vehicle just before the stream gives evidence that the trail was originally a jeep road built during World War II. Usually, the trail

along the stream is wet and muddy. Some ample swimming holes in the stream provide some relief from the heat and places to clean up, particularly on the return hike. About ½ mile from the trailhead, turn right onto the trail that ascends the south side of the ridge until it meets an old irrigation ditch. The trail to the right leads to the now-closed trailhead of what was once called the "Upper Ditch Trail." Go left on the trail paralleling the irrigation ditch until it reaches a dam and an irrigation tunnel after 2 miles. At the tunnel, which is no longer used, the trail switchbacks up to the crest of a ridge overlooking Waimano Stream. For the next mile, the trail follows the ridge above the stream. You can expect to find some generous pools to swim in, if you wish to scramble down the hillside to them. A dam just before the confluence of Waimano Stream and a smaller stream entering from the right mark the point where you start to ascend the ridge which leads to the Koolau summit.

The lower valley contains two of the most noble trees on the island. The kukui (*Aleurites moluccana*), or candlenut tree, a massive tree with maplelike leaves and black, walnut-sized nuts, was one of the most important trees to the island's economy. Kukui-nut oil was burned in stone lamps, the nuts were made into leis and a variety of costume jewelry, and the trunk was used to make canoes. The monkey-pod tree (*Samanea saman*) will commonly grow to 80 feet. It is a symmetrical tree with tiny, delicate, pink tufts when in bloom, and tiny, fernlike leaflets. From the handsome wood, beautiful and highly prized bowls and trays are made. Both trees as well as the familiar hau tree are conspicuous in the valley.

From the last dam, the trail climbs 1600 feet to summit. This is the most difficult part of the trail. Since the path here is overgrown in places, it is a good idea to wear long pants and a shirt. Periodically, you will have good views of Waimano Valley to the north (left) and of Waiau (lit., "swirling water") Valley to the south (right). However, the highlight of the hike, and the primary reason for making it, is to stand at the summit high above Waihee (lit., "squid liquid") Valley to the east. You will encounter strong winds at the summit. If rain or clouds obstruct your view, be patient, for the winds usually blow the obstruction away quickly.

On the Papali Trail

MANANA

(Hiking Area No. 18)

Rating: Difficult.

Features: Views from the Koolau Mountain Range, native and introduced flora.

Permission: None.

Hiking Distance & Time: 6 miles, 4 hours, 1700-foot gain.

Driving Instructions: From Honolulu (15 miles, ½ hour) drive northwest on H-1 to Pearl City (Exit 10), bear right on Moanalua Road to its end, then right on Waimano Home Road (.7 mile), and finally left on Komo Mai Drive to the end.

Bus Instructions: From Ala Moana Center take bus #53 (Pacific Palisades) to Pearl City Shopping Center (Kamehameha Highway and Waimano Home Road intersection). Transfer to Pearlridge-Pearl City Shuttle bus and take to Komo Mai Drive. Walk up Komo Mai Drive to trailhead.

Introductory Notes: The Manana Trail is one of a number of trails (Hiking Area Nos. 17, 19 and 21) which take you to peaks atop the Koolau Mountain Range. This trail is little traveled and is overgrown in places, and should be attempted only by skilled hikers. (It is possible to connect with the Waimano Trail by following the cliffs to the south, but the connecting route is very dangerous and not advised.) Rain and mud are frequently encountered in this relatively pristine place. If you are looking for solitude and for the joys as well as the trials present in a rainforest, then Manana will satisfy you.

On the Trail: A paved pedestrian passageway leads .4 mile to a water tank. Strawberry guava is abundant along this portion of the trail. From the tank, the Manana Trail climbs 1700 feet to a peak atop the Koolau Range. Eucalyptus, guava and koa trees are abundant along the lower part of the trail, where they are struggling to overcome the ravages of a severe fire in 1972. For your protection, stay on the ridgeline and avoid the side trails, most of which lead to Manana Stream to the north (left) or Waimano Stream to the south. Time permitting, you may wish to hike to Manana Stream for a swim. If so, it would be a good idea to mark your route down so you can follow it back.

In addition to the trees previously noted, look for the sandalwood tree (*Santalum freycinetianum*), with narrow, pointed, shiny leaves. Once an important source of income for the islands, the wood was exported for use in furniture and for its oil and perfume. In fact, China imported so much sandalwood that the Chinese once called Hawaii the "Sandalwood Islands."

A variety of ferns and low scrub dominate the upper part of the trail and seem to reach out to scratch and cut the legs and arms, so protective clothing is well-advised. Strong winds greet the hiker at the summit, but with any luck the air is clear, so that the views into Kaalaea (lit., "the ocherous earth") Valley can be enjoyed. A return via the Waimano Trail is possible for the daring and skilled hiker. The 1-mile hike south to it along the cliffs is extremely dangerous, and a miscalculation could drop the hiker 1500 feet or more to the valley below. Caution is well-advised.

WAHIAWA
(Hiking Area No. 19)

Rating: Strenuous.

Features: Views from the Koolau Mountain Range, native and introduced flora, swimming.

Permission: (1) Secure hiking permit from Division of Forestry. (2) Access permit from U.S. Army, Range Control. Military requires 30-day advance written notice.

Hiking Distance & Time: 4 miles, 3 hours, 650-foot gain.

Driving Instructions: From Honolulu (22 miles, 1 hour) drive northwest on H-1, then right on H-2 to Wahiawa exit. Bear right on Route 80 into Wahiawa and right on California Ave. From the Route 80/California Ave. junction, it is 5 miles to the trailhead. At the end of the Wahiawa Homestead, California Ave. makes a right turn and shortly a left. A few hundred yards down the road on the right there is a gate to the Schofield Barracks East Range. Enter the range land, make a quick left and follow the dirt road for 2 miles until it makes a sharp turn to the right to return to Wahiawa.

Bus Instructions: From Ala Moana Center take bus #52 (Wahiawa/Circle Island) to Wahiawa and to California Ave. Walk up California Ave. to the trailhead, 5 miles.

Introductory Notes: This is the easiest hike to the Koolau Mountain Range crest (See Hiking Area Nos. 17, 18 and 21). However, permission from the military is troublesome to secure. It usually takes three days to get a permit to enter the military reservation,

and the trail is usually available to hike only on weekends and on holidays when the range is not in use.
Write ahead, and good luck.

On the Trail: The trail begins at the apex of the
abrupt right turn on the dirt road. Also known as the
Schofield-Waikane Trail, the Wahiawa (lit., "milkfish
place") Trail parallels the military-reservation boundary and travels between the north and south forks of
Kaikonahua (probably, "fat place") Stream. This
33-mile‑long stream is the longest in the State.
Damage caused by the 1970 Kipapa (lit., "placed
prone") fire is evident along the first part of the trail.
A short distance from the trailhead (.4 mile) a trail
descends north (left) to the north fork of Kaikonahua Stream, along which you can find a number of
swimming holes. The stream is 400 vertical feet and
.4 miles below the main trail but is worth a side trip
to visit and to swim in.

Ohia lehua, ohia ha, naupaka and olapa are a few
of the native plants found along the trail. The olapa
(*Cheirodendron gaudichaudii*) is a native mountain
tree from which early Hawaiians cut poles. They put
a sticky, gummy substance on one end of a pole to
catch birds for their feathers. Bird feathers were highly prized, particularly by Hawaiian royalty for making garments. Another tree, ohia ha (*Syzygium sand-
wicense*) played an important part in early Hawaii.
The hard and durable reddish wood was used for
house timbers and paddles. It is a large tree whose
reddish-brown, smooth bark yielded a black dye.

The trail follows the ridgeline, dipping between
saddles until it reaches the summit at 2400 feet.
From high above the floor of Kahana Valley 1500
feet below, the views of the east side are superb.
However, as is usually the condition all along the
Koolau pali, strong winds buffet the hiker here.

Trail . . . .
Jeep Road - - - -

POAMOHO VALLEY

(Hiking Area No. 20)

Rating: Hardy family.

Features: Introduced and native flora, swimming.

Permission: (1) Hiking permit from Division of Forestry. (2) Access permit from U.S. Army, Range Control. Military requires 30-day advance written notice.

Hiking Distance & Time: 3 miles, 2 hours, 1000-foot gain.

Driving Instructions: From Honolulu (22 miles, 1 hour) drive northwest on H-1, then right on H-2 to the end of the freeway just south of Wahiawa. Bear right on Route 80 into Wahiawa and right on Whitmore Ave. (Route 804) to its end, then continue on a jeep road to its end by an abandoned shack.

Bus Instructions: From Ala Moana Center take bus #52 (Wahiawa/Circle Island) to Wahiawa and to California Ave. Walk north on Kamehameha Highway and then right on Whitmore Ave. 2 miles to the trailhead.

Introductory Notes: The hike into Poamoho Valley is rough and wet. There is no trail, so the hiker must follow the stream and do a lot of rock-hopping. However, that is the joy of the hike. There are numerous swimming holes and places to splash and to picnic.

On the Trail: The trail descends a short distance to the north (left) of the shack, and joins Poamoho Stream near a gauging station. Since the valley was once the site of a plantation arboretum, the hiker is treated to a great variety of introduced and native flora. The former includes eucalyptus and paper bark and the latter includes koa and kukui trees. Paper bark (*Melaleuca leucadendra*) is an interesting tree, characterized by a bark that peels off in sheets that are very much like paper.

The valley alternately narrows and widens as we hike east. After 2 miles, look for a spur trail which leads north (left) up the cliffs to join the Poamoho Ridge Trail. From this junction, you may choose to hike the Poamoho Ridge Trail to the ridge along the Koolau Range, which is 1.5 miles and 1000 feet of elevation gain distant. If not, the stream trail continues into the valley for another mile. After that, large boulders and thick vegetation make hiking difficult and dangerous.

POAMOHO RIDGE
(Hiking Area No. 21)

Rating: Strenuous.

Features: Views from the Koolau Mountain Range, native and introduced flora, camping.

Permission: (1) Hiking, camping and shelter-use permit from Division of Forestry. (2) Access permit from U.S. Army, Range Control. (3) Access permit from Dole Pineapple Co. (4) Access permit from Waialua Sugar Company. Twenty-four-hour advance notice required. Military requires 30-day advance written notice.

Hiking Distance & Time: 3.4 miles, 3 hours, 800-foot gain.

Driving Instructions: From Honolulu (28 miles 1½ hours) drive northwest on H-1, then right on H-2 to the end of the freeway just south of Wahiawa. Bear left on Route 99 to the Dole Pineapple stand north of Wahiawa. Turn right on a dirt road just past the stand and follow it to the trailhead (5.5 miles). First you circle to the right around the U.S. Army Helemano Radio Station and then turn right past a water tank through a pineapple field and then through a cane field to the Forest Reserve boundary. The last 2 miles are on a rough jeep road along the ridge to the trailhead.

Bus Instructions: From Ala Moana Center take bus #52 (Wahiawa/Circle Island) to the Dole Pineapple stand north of Wahiawa. Walk north to the road past the stand and follow the road to the trailhead, 5.5 miles.

Introductory Notes: Securing permission for this hike is complicated and takes a few days. Additionally, the trail is ordinarily open only on weekends and on holidays. Time permitting, make the effort, for this is a delightful hike over some little-traveled terrain.

On the Trail: The trail begins east of the parking area
at the end of the road and follows the main ridge
until it reaches the summit of the Koolau Mountain
Range. Avoid the hunting trails that lead off the main
ridge, for many simply lead into the brush or loop to
rejoin the ridge trail. At the 1.5-mile point, you can
hike south (right) a short distance down into the valley to Poamoho Stream. There are a few swimming
spots and places to picnic along it. A number of
native trees can be identified along the ridge and in
the valley, such as ohia, koa and kawau. The kawau
(*Byronia sandwicensis*), or Hawaiian holly tree, is
distinguised by grayish-yellow wood, white blossoms
and black berries.

A surprise awaits the hiker at the summit: the
viewpoint here has a generous, flat, grassy area. From
its east end one has magnificent views of Punaluu
Valley and Kahana Valley to the southeast. In the
absence of rain or fog, the summit is a delightful
place to find solitude as well as a panorama of the island. A short hike (0.2 mile) south (right) along the
summit trail leads to an overnight Forest Reserve
cabin. Although the shelter does not provide any
amenities, the alternative to spending overnight in it
is to tent on the wet ground and to endure nightly
rains and wind.

DUPONT

(Hiking Area No. 22)

Rating: Difficult (and dangerous).

Features: Views from the highest point on Oahu (4,025 feet), forest and pasture land, native flora.

Permission: (1) Hiking permit from Division of Forestry. (2) Liability waiver from Waialua Sugar Company. (3) Permit from Waialua Ranch Partners. Twenty-four-hour advance notice required from all above.

Hiking Distance & Time: 4 miles, 5 hours, 3800-foot gain.

Driving Instructions: From Honolulu (30 miles, 1½ hours) drive northwest on H-1, then right on H-2 to end of freeway (completed to Wahiawa at time of writing). Continue on Route 99 to a traffic circle, where you bear left on Route 930 west to Waialua and to Waialua High School. Go left on a cane road just past the school. Drive 1.5 miles up road and park by the second gate.

Bus Instructions: From Ala Moana Center take bus #52 (Wahiawa/Circle Island) to Wahiawa and to California Ave. Transfer to bus #76 (Waialua/Haleiwa) and take it to the Goodale Ave./Farrington Highway junction in Waialua. Walk or hitchhike west on the highway to the trailhead.

Introductory Notes: Mt. Kaala (probably, "to hurl stones with a sling") is noteworthy for at least two reasons; it is the highest point on Oahu and the ascent of it is the most difficult hike on the island. The last mile of the hike is very dangerous, and requires skill and a stout heart. Parts of this trail require the hiker to scramble, climb and crawl along narrow ledges with a 2000-foot drop into the valley below. (Ropes have been placed to aid hikers in the most difficult

To Kaena Point

Waialua

930

High School

To Honolulu

N
W — E
S

Forest Reserve Boundary

Mokuleia Forest Reserve

F.A.A. Road

Kaala 4,025' Satellite Station

Trail · · · ·
Jeep Road - - - -

places.) If heights are a problem for you, DO NOT attempt this hike. This is not a hike for timid people! You can reach the summit via a longer route on roads.

On the Trail: The Dupont Trail begins beyond the second gate, where the road makes a right turn. Proceed straight ahead on the jeep road a short distance until you reach a gate that secures the pasture land, where the jeep road turns right. From here, Mt. Kaala, distinguished by the white, domed radio and radar installations, is to your front-left while Kaupakuhale (lit., "house ridgepole or roof") Ridge is to your front-right. You must hike cross-county up Kaupakuhale Ridge. There is no trail until you reach the Forest Reserve boundary 1.3 miles distant. Therefore, you should walk toward the ridge through the pasture land and over a few small hills. What appear to be trails are simply cattle contours, which will lead you in circles if you follow them. A fence and a locked gate on the ridge mark the beginning of the foot trail through the Mokuleia (lit., "isle of abundance") Forest Reserve.

Trailhead, Dupont Trail

The difference between the pasture and the forest is apparent. The forest part of the trail passes through heavy foliage, which periodically obscures the trail. However, the ridge begins to narrow considerably, and the danger does not lie in losing the trail but rather in stumbling or sliding off the ridge. A variety of native plants is evident in the forest. Ohia, with its bright red flowers, and hapuu (*Cibotium chamissoi*), or Hawaiian tree fern, are plentiful. The most notable use of the tree fern has been the carving of tikis (carved representation of ancestors) from the trunk. In times of famine, the stems and the core of the trunk have been used for food.

As you ascend, the ridge will alternately narrow and widen. Be cautious and alert, particularly in those places where the footing is composed of loose and brittle volcanic rock. Pause frequently to study the trail ahead and to enjoy the views of the north side of the island and of the deep and startling valleys and gulches on each side of the ridge. The last 1 mile climbs 1800 feet and is the most dangerous part of the hike. Ropes have been placed at the most difficult and the narrowest parts of the ridge. BE CERTAIN to test these ropes to determine whether they will support your weight. Indeed, you may wish to pause and consider returning down the trail rather than risking the difficult ascent ahead.

Abruptly, the trail meets a paved road, which will take you to the summit ¼ mile away. Federal officials do not welcome visitors to the radio and radar facilities at the summit, as numerous "no trespassing" signs attest. Mt. Kaala presides over the island at 4,025 feet. The summit is a mile-wide plateau containing a montane bog which has been considerably altered by building over the years. On a clear day, the views of the island, particularly those to the west, are overwhelming. Makaha Valley lies at your feet, and

Military installations on Mt. Kaala

the sweep of the coastline to Kaena Point is sufficient reward for your efforts.

From the summit you may choose to follow the road instead of returning via the trail. It is 8.3 miles to Farrington Highway. If you're lucky, you might get a ride in one of the service vehicles or with the personnel who work at the summit installation. Hawaiian raspberries (*Rubus hawaiiensis*) are abundant along the road, and although the dark berries are edible, they can be rather bitter.

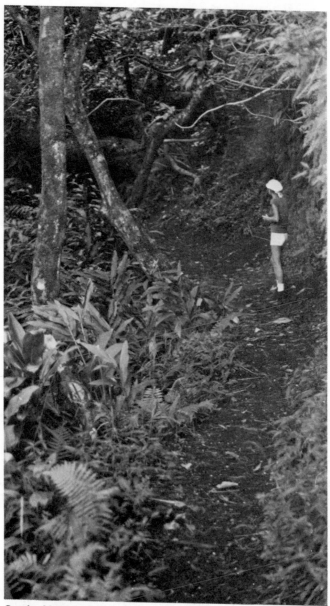

On the Manoa Cliffs Trail

KANEAKI HEIAU

(Hiking Area No. 23)

Rating: Family.

Features: Kaneaki Heiau, fruits, native and introduced flora.

Permission: Access from 10 a.m. to 2 p.m. every day.

Hiking Distance & Time: .5 mile, ½ hour.

Driving Instructions: From Honolulu (36 miles, 1½ hours) drive northwest on H-1, which becomes Route 93 when the freeway ends. In Makaha, go toward the Makaha Inn, go right on Huipu and right on Maunaolu St. to Alahele St.; turn left to the end of the road and a parking area outside the Heiau.

Bus Instructions: From Ala Moana Center take bus
#51 (Makaha) to Makaha, then follow the driving
instructions above—on foot.

Introductory Notes: If you are on the leeward side of
the island, it is worth a visit. Today, Makaha (lit.,
"fierce") Valley is rapidly developing into a tourist
center. Historically, Makaha was noted for robbers
and for cannibals, although there is some question
whether people there really cannibalized.

On the Trail: From the parking area follow the road
for about 50 feet to a footpath on the right which
leads directly to the heiau, a pre-Christian place of
worship. Kaneaki, restored in 1969-70, is one of the
best-preserved heiaus on Oahu. Built in the 13th
Century, Kaneaki was first used as a temple for
agricultural worship. It later became a temple to the
god of war. A number of structures and ceremonial
sites have been reconstructed, identified by interpretive signs. For example, there are the hale-pahu, or
drum house, and the hale-mana, or house of spiritual
power, from which the Kahunas ("priests") received
power. There are also a lele ("altar"), a number of
kikis ("images") and two anuus, or towers of worship. A stroll through the heiau provides some insight
into the role played by these important religious and
cultural places.

An array of native and introduced flora enhances
the beauty of the heiau and of Makaha (lit., "fierce")
Valley. Two fruits are readily available. Papaya
(*Carica papaya*) is found growing in clusters at the
bases of umbrellalike leaves. Yellow when ripe, the
sweet papaya fruit is usually the size of a squash and
is a favorite of visitors and locals. Guava is also plentiful, so choose the ripest of these yellow, lemon-
sized fruits. A shower of color is provided by red and

white hibiscus—the Hawaii state flower—crotons, with their multicolored leaves, and the striking heliconia (*Heliconia humilis*), or lobster claw. The bright red bracts of this flower, which resemble the claw of a boiled lobster, are used by practitioners of ikebana—flower arranging. Shade in this area is provided by towering kukui trees.

Tiki at Kaneaki Heiau

KUAOKALA

(Hiking Area No. 24)

Rating: Strenuous. Elevation gain 500 feet.

Features: Views of mountain and coastal area, fruits, camping.

Permission: Permit to hike and to camp from Division of Forestry.

Hiking Distance & Time: 4½-mile loop, 3 hours.

Driving Instructions:

From Honolulu (41 miles, 2 hours) drive northwest on H-1, which becomes Route 93 when the freeway ends. Drive past Makua town to a military road and a guard shack on the right just before the end of the paved road. Go right on the military road and check in at the guard shack. Drive 2.6 miles on the military road to the designated parking area.

Bus Instructions:

From Ala Moana Center take Bus #51 (Honolulu-

Makaha) to the end of the line near the surfing beach north of Makaha. Walk or hitchhike to the military road and guard shack.

Introductory Notes: A good hike, solitude and magnificent views are what you will find in the Kuaokala (lit., "back of the sun") Forest Reserve. The access road is under military jurisdiction, so permits are a must.

On the Trail: The trailhead and the designated parking place are one and the same. If you look back about 100 yards along the road you drove on and then to the left to a water tank, you will see the point at which you will emerge from the loop hike. The route descends on the paved road next to the parking area and continues on a dirt jeep road for 2.8 miles. The paved part of the road is lined with guava trees whose fruit is some of the sweetest I have ever eaten. These lemon-sized fruits are yellow and soft when ripe. The trail makes a number of dips and turns in and out of small gulches which are heavily shaded by eucalyptus, pine, and cypress trees. After about one mile the trail ascends a ridge over open country and then reaches a number of points from which panoramas are possible of the saddle area between the two mountain ranges of Oahu, of the Koolau Mountains to the east and of the north shore. These viewpoints are pleasant places to pause. From the second vista point, at a gate and cattle guard, look to the front across a gulch to the ridge at the head of the gulch. You will be hiking along that ridge overlooking Makua Valley. From the second vista point, the trail makes a steep descent and snakes over the gulch's floor before ascending to the ridgeline. Just before the ridge, at the 2.6-mile point at a turnout on the left, the remains of the Kuaokala shack are partly visible through the tall grass. From here, the foot trail is just 0.2 mile. A short distance from the abandoned shack, you reach a four-road junction. Follow the road to the front-right a short distance to a turnout which was once the start of a jeep road and which leads uphill to a group of eucalyptus trees. At this point you have your first view of Makua (lit., "parents") Valley.

The footpath part of the Kuaokala Trail begins to the right from the viewpoint overlooking Makua Valley and descends west along the north ridge above Makua Valley. After a descent, the trail ascends to a perch 1800 feet above the Makua Valley floor, where views of the valley and the west coast of Oahu are outstanding. Then the trail makes another descent and begins to turn north through open forest. The "golf ball" at the Kaena Point Satellite Tracking Station at the trailhead is now visible. The trail continues a circuitous path through the forest until it reaches a trail junction at the 4.0-mile point. The spur trail straight ahead ascends a short distance to a viewpoint, and the main trail turns to the right. Take the spur trail and enjoy the views. It is a good lunch spot. Return to the main trail and follow it to the water tank. Then walk down the paved road from the tank to the main road and turn right to reach the trailhead.

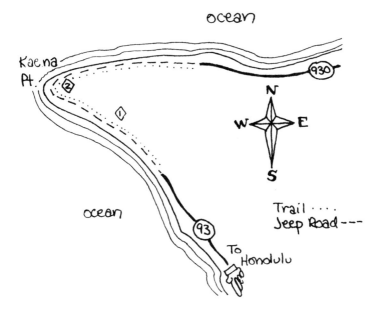

KAENA POINT

(Hiking Area No. 25)

Rating: Hardy family.

Features: Views of coastal area, tidepools, swimming.

Permission: None.

Hiking Distance & Time: 2 miles, 1½ hours.

Driving Instructions: From Honolulu (42 miles, 2 hours) drive northwest on H-2, which becomes Route 93 when the freeway ends. Drive past Makua town to the end of the paved road as far as you dare. Large holes and dirt barriers make passage difficult even for four-wheel-drive vehicles.

Bus Instructions: From Ala Moana Center take bus #51 (Makaha) to the end of the line and walk or hitchhike to the end of the road.

Introductory Notes: The trade winds and the ocean offer some relief along this hot and dusty hike. Instead of the west shore, you may choose to hike to Kaena Point along the north shore, if you are camping at Mokuleia or touring in that area.

On the Trail: The trail begins from the point to which you dare to drive. You may hike the road, which follows the coastline, or walk along the shore, where you can splash to cool off and can investigate tidepools and the collection of debris washed onto shore. You are likely to find local people fishing, snorkeling and throwing nets. Visit with them and check out their catch. I have never known a local to be "skunked" fishing. The thorny kiawe tree dominates the area, but its growth is usually stunted due to the lack of water.

Legends abound concerning Kaena (lit., "the heat") Point. One legend claims that the demigod Maui cast his giant hook from here to the island of Kauai in an attempt to join Oahu and Kauai. He hooked Kauai and gave a tremendous tug. A rock broke off and landed at his feet, while his hook sailed over his head and landed in Palolo Valley, making Kaau Crater (see Hiking Area No. 9). The farther of two islets off Kaena Point, Pohaku-o-Kauai (lit., "rock of Kauai"), is said to be the rock that was broken off from Kauai by Maui. Another legend regarding this islet tells of Haupu, a great warrior from Kauai who had a short temper. It seems that the noise from a hukilau, or fishing party, being held on the point so disturbed Haupu that he hurled this huge rock, killing many people. There is no legend regarding the other, somewhat smaller islet, named Pohaku-o-Oahu (lit., "rock of Oahu"), which is closer to shore.

Legend aside, Kaena Point was an important place in pre-Christian religious belief. It was thought to be the place where the souls of Hawaiian dead began their journey to Kahiki—the immortal land of their ancestors. A white rock about .4 mile offshore was believed to be the exact point from which the soul made its leap to the Other World. The rock is called Leina Kauhane (lit., "leaping place of ghosts").

Coast near Kaena Point

Appendix

Division of State Parks
1151 Punchbowl St.
Room 310
Honolulu, Oahu 96813
Tel. 548-7455

1. camping permit for
   state park
2. hiking permit for
   Diamond Head

Zions Securities Corp.
Laie Shopping Center
55-510 Kamehameha Highway
Laie, Oahu 96762
Tel. 293-9201

1. hiking permit for
   Laie (No. 15)

Division of Forestry
1151 Punchbowl St.
Room 325
Honolulu, Oahu 96813
Tel. 548-2861

1. hiking permits
2. camping and
   shelter use permits

U.S. Army Support Comm.
Real Property Branch
Tel. 655-4954

1. access permit

Dole Pineapple Co.
Tel. 621-5052

1. access permit

Waialua Sugar Co.
Waialua, Oahu 96786
Tel. 637-3521

1. access permit

Waialua Ranch Partners
Tel. 637-9441
Mr. Bob Cherry

1. access permit

Department of Parks and
   Recreation
Honolulu Municipal Building
Honolulu, Oahu 96813
Tel. 523-4525

1. camping permits

OR from Satellite City Halls:

Kaneohe
46-018 Kam Hwy.
Kaneohe, Oahu 96744
Tel. 235-4571

Kailua
302 Kuulei Rd.
Kailua, Oahu 96734
Tel. 261-8575

Wahiawa
830 California Ave.
Wahiawa, Oahu 96786
Tel. 621-0791

Waianae
85-555 Farrington Hwy.
Waianae, Oahu 96792
Tel. 696-6371

Beretania
1290 Aala St.
Honolulu, Oahu 96817
Tel. 523-2405

Kalihi
1865 Kam IV Road
Honolulu, Oahu 96819
Tel. 847-4688

Hawaii Kai
2nd Floor
Koko Marina Shopping Center
Honolulu, Oahu 96825
Tel. 395-4418

Ewa
91-923 Ft. Weaver Road
Ewa Beach, Oahu 96706
Tel. 689-7914

Waipahu
Waipahu Shopping Plaza
Tel. 671-5638

Hauula
Hauula Kai Shopping Center
54-316 Kam Hwy.
Tel. 293-8551

Index

Other Books From Wilderness Press

Wilderness Press publishes many other fine outdoor books. The complete list is below. Write for a free catalog.

Arizona Trails	Sierra Nevada Flora
Backpackers Sourcebook	Sierra North
Backpacking Basics	Sierra South
Bicycling in Hawaii	The Anza-Borrego Desert Region
Hawaiian Camping	The Boundary Waters Canoe Area
Hiking Hawaii	The John Muir Trail
Hiking Kauai	The Pacific Crest Trail
Hiking Maui	The Tahoe Sierra
Hiking Oahu	The Tahoe-Yosemite Trail
Huckleberry Country	Trails of the Angeles
Lassen Volcanic National Park	The Vertical World of Yosemite
Marble Mountain Wilderness	Waxing for Cross-Country Skiing
A Pacific Crest Odyssey	Wild Food Plants of the Sierra
Point Reyes	Yosemite Climber
San Bernardino Mountain Trails	Yosemite National Park

Desolation Wilderness and the South Lake Tahoe Basin
Guide to the Golden Gate National Recreation Area
Nordic Touring and Cross-Country Skiing
Outdoor Guide to the San Francisco Bay Area
Self-Propelled in the Southern Sierra
The Cross-Country Ski, Cook, Look and Pleasure Book
The Sawtooth National Recreation Area

PLUS hiking guides to all the 15-minute quadrangles in the High Sierra, such as **Tuolumne Meadows, Mineral King** and **Mt. Whitney**.

Wilderness Press

2440 bancroft way · berkeley, california 94704